LEE²

LEE TO THE POWER OF TWO

LEE²

JAMES KNIGHT

with

Shane & Brett Lee

HarperSports
An imprint of HarperCollinsPublishers

Harper*Sports*

An imprint of HarperCollins*Publishers*, Australia

First published in Australia by HarperCollins*Publishers* Pty Limited
ABN 36 009 913 517
A member of the HarperCollins*Publishers* (Australia) Pty Limited Group
www.harpercollins.com.au

HarperCollins*Publishers*

25 Ryde Road, Pymble, Sydney, NSW 2073, Australia
31 View Road, Glenfield, Auckland 10, New Zealand
77–85 Fulham Palace Road, London W6 8JB, United Kingdom
Hazelton Lanes, 55 Avenue Road, Suite 2900, Toronto, Ontario M5R 3L2
and 1995 Markham Road, Scarborough, Ontario M1B 5M8, Canada
10 East 53rd Street, New York, NY 10022, USA

National Library of Australia Cataloguing-in-Publication data:

Knight, James, 1967– .
Lee2: Lee to the power of two.
ISBN 0 7322 6924 5.
1. Lee, Shane. 2. Lee, Brett. 3. Cricket players –
Australia – Biography. I. Lee, Shane. II. Lee, Brett.
796.358092

Front and back cover photographs by Michelle Wilson
Cover and internal design by Luke Causby, HarperCollins Design Studio
Typeset by HarperCollins Design Studio in 11.5 on 16pt Bembo
Printed and bound in Australia by Griffin Press on 79gsm Bulky Paperback

5 4 3 2 1   01 02 03 04

To Mum, Dad, and Grant.
Thank you for your love, guidance and support
every step of the journey.
— Shane and Brett

To Mum, Pete and Ando.
'We made it!'
— James

Acknowledgments

The author would like to thank Bob Lee, Helen Lee, Grant Lee, Jamie Annetts, Richard Bowman, Richard Chee Quee, Graeme Creighton, Phil Emery, David Freedman, Brad Haddin, Bruce Jones, Dennis Lillee, Brad McNamara, Neil Maxwell, Fiona Melvin, Kerry Penfold, Garth Porter, Adam Rainford, Corey Richards and Gavin Robertson.

Thank you to HarperCollins for giving me the biggest thrill of my working life. With special thanks to Alison Urquhart, Vanessa Radnidge, Melanie Cain, Karen-Maree Griffiths, Luke Causby, Graeme Jones and Cheryl Rose. A great team.

Contents

PROLOGUE

6.00 p.m., Wednesday 17th May.
The Sound Level Recording and Rehearsal Studios
Pyrmont, Sydney

The room smells of sweat and dust. Its walls are foam-padded, electrical cords wind across the floor, and empty Coke bottles stand at attention on a window sill. For five mates, this is a world very different from their usual day-to-day one. A world of late nights, bleary eyes, hoarse voices and headaches. The world of the muso.

'One, two, three!' yells Riddler. He clicks his drumsticks together, and Studio 5 bursts alive to a cover version of 'All the Small Things', a popular song from the in-your-face American band, Blink 182.

Riddler, a soaked T-shirt clinging to his back, has spent the past four days in bed with a virus. His voice matches his weary look. Buzzard, the lead guitarist, stands to the right of Riddler. The only person in the room without a microphone, he quietly strums the strings, mouth firmly shut, eyes occasionally roving the room. Cheeks, the lead vocalist, moves rhythmically, tracksuit legs shaking, and sandals tapping.

The remaining two band members strum their guitars side by side. They are pictures of concentration, every finger movement from chord to chord is closely watched. Their blond heads nod in time with the beat. They glance briefly at each other, then lean into the microphones, singing, 'Work sux, I know.'

They grin, then their foreheads begin to crease as they concentrate again on their fingers until the song winds down.

'We missed the last two,' Riddler croaks, shaking his head.

'Someone's out,' adds Buzzard. Cheeks takes a swig of his Coke and swallows quickly. 'Let's do it again. From the top,' he suggests.

The conversation bounces around the room for a few minutes until it's decided that the two blond guitarists will play a section of the music together to work out who's hitting the wrong chord.

The younger, shorter and thinner blond is playing bass, an electric-blue strap hangs over his shoulder. He is dressed in a dark-blue singlet, white shorts, and sports shoes. Unlike the members of Blink 182 whose bodies are heavily engraved with tattoos, the only blemishes on this muso's skin are two small knife nicks near his heels, the results of recent surgery to remove spurs from the backs of his ankles. He shows no sign of any pain as he taps to the beat.

The older, taller, and broader blond is on rhythm guitar. He wears a grey T-shirt, black jeans and leather shoes. He walks forward a step, back a step in a ceaseless pattern until two contrasting notes scar the air. Riddler hurriedly points his drumsticks: 'Stop! Yeh, that's it there.' Both blonds stop.

The younger one takes the lead: 'It's gotta go C, G, click, click, back to an F. "Say it ain't so." C, G, click, click, back to an F.'

The older one nods: 'That's where I went wrong. I was hitting the F too early.'

'Well let's get it right,' says the younger one. 'It'll sound shit if we don't get it right on the weekend.'

The weekend. Just 48 hours away. So much to do, so little time. This band of five is racing against the clock to be ready for a

Friday night gig at the Ettamogah Hotel at Campbelltown in Sydney's south-west. And then there's Saturday night at the Castle Hill Tavern. They've already been practising for three hours, only one more to go until their time is up, and the more hardened musos begin rolling in.

'Let's go again,' urges Riddler, anxiety pressing down on his eyebrows. 'One, two, three.' The drumsticks click again.

'All the small things ...'

The song begins well, but all five know the test lies ahead. Feet continue tapping, vocal chords strain. Then, the moment arrives. Will it be C,G click, click, back to an F? Or will the band be tormented again? Riddler's mouth opens, Buzzard stares ahead, Cheeks looks sideways.

C,G, click, click, back to an F.

YES! Not a stray or mistimed note to be heard. Riddler smiles, Buzzard nods, Cheeks throws his voice full throttle into the chorus. This is music to their ears.

The two blonds continue frowning in concentration until the song ends, then it's time to relax, and the older one smirks.

'Well that one's in the can.' He laughs, a half-throated chuckle. 'What's next?'

'All Torn Down?' offers Cheeks.

Riddler shakes his head. 'No, we can do that one. Let's do "Prisoner".'

'Shit here we go, this'll test us,' says the older blond.

'Do "Ballroom Blitz" first,' replies Cheeks.

Riddler nods and the familiar clicking of sticks fires up the band again. Cheeks chokes the microphone, and rocks the stand backwards into his chest; his eyes dart from Riddler to Buzzard. The three of them have an association that began long before they struck a musical allegiance: Cheeks, a thumping opening batsman; Buzzard, a hard-nosed all-rounder; and Riddler, an off-spinner, all played cricket together for New South Wales. Riddler even managed four Test matches and 13 one-dayers for Australia.

From the flannelled friendships the band, Six and Out, was formed, an obvious name considering the cricketing heritage, but perhaps 'Hat-trick' is just as appropriate because the blond guitarists have a habit of reducing the group to three while joining another band of players on domestic and international tours. However, on their return, they are always welcomed back into Six and Out. No hard feelings at all.

Cheeks, microphone stand still resting against his chest, turns his attention to the blonds.

'OK, "Ballroom Blitz". Are you ready Lee?'

'I'm ready.'

'B. Lee?'

'Always ready.'

CHAPTER ONE

NO ORDINARY LIFE

I went to the press conference, and there were cameras
everywhere. I thought this is it. This is what I have to get
used to. I did enjoy it, but it frightened me at first.

Brett Lee recalling his first media conference
as an Australian player

Helen Lee and her nephew Luke sat at the living-room table and sifted through the mountain of fan mail that had gathered over the 1999–2000 summer. Luke reached for a small parcel. What was inside? Was it another invitation for his cousin Brett to partner a schoolgirl to her end-of-year formal? A photograph? A poem? A simple card with well wishes?

No. Not this time. This latest gift was a pair of pantyhose addressed to the newest heart-throb in Australian sport. Perhaps the sender had been inspired by the clichéd practice of fans hurling underwear at Welsh singing superstar Tom Jones whenever he walked onto a stage. Maybe the action had been prompted by Dutch courage. Or was it to win a bet? Whatever the reason, the unexpected arrival of the nylon legs was just another sign, albeit an unusual one, that Brett had joined his brother Shane not only on the music stage, but on the stage reserved for those in the spotlight.

Since the early 1990s the brothers from Mount Warrigal on the New South Wales South Coast have left significant impressions on Australia's sporting public:

There's a touch of Shane Warne about Shane Lee. Never mind for a moment their cricket. Lee, 20, is a fresh face who today begins only his third Sheffield Shield match against South Australia at the Sydney Cricket Ground. He bowls speed, not bewitching leggies, bats and fields better than Warne and comes from Wollongong.

What the pair share is charisma. Like Warne, Lee excites the imagination. Blond and burly with a powerful bowling action and a capacity to strike the ball as hard as any contemporary, Lee is the type cricket needs. (Daniel Williams, *Sydney Morning Herald*, 16 February 1994)

Lee [Brett] appears as dashing and uncluttered as one of those chaps from *Home and Away* over whom the pommies swoon. And is there not a glint in his eye that suggests he enjoys the spotlight more than is usual in a fellow born and properly raised in the bush? (Peter Roebuck, *Sydney Morning Herald*, 26 December 1999)

The Lee brothers. If they were able to travel in a time machine and be given the choice of playing cricket in any era, it's hard to imagine them choosing anywhere but the present. They are modern-day cricketers. Gold bracelets, vogue hairstyles, smart clothes. Smooth, slick, snappy.

And yet, their highly publicised international debuts rekindled memories of bygone times. Was Shane to be the next Simon O'Donnell? Perhaps dig deeper into the memory and compare him with Keith Miller, Alan Davidson or Richie Benaud. The pressure and expectations were enormous on a 22-year-old who'd just walked from the Adelaide Oval on 17 December 1995 after stunning the West Indies with a whirlwind 39 off 27 balls in a preliminary Benson and Hedges World Series match. He later took Jimmy Adams' wicket in a tidy return of 1–20 off 7 overs as the Australians strolled to a 121-run victory. It had been a memorable start for Shane, but in hindsight he believes he wasn't prepared for his sudden rise:

It all happened so quickly. I was in Coffs Harbour for a country cup promotional game for New South Wales. Things had been going pretty well for me in the Mercantile Mutual Cup, I'd strung together a few good games, but I certainly wasn't expecting anything more. Then I received a call from Neil Maxwell at the NSW Cricket offices back in Sydney. He said I'd been picked in the Australian team and had to go to Adelaide in the morning to prepare for the game against the West Indies. I questioned Maxey first and said: 'Bullshit, you're kidding aren't you?' But he assured me he'd got the call from the Australian Cricket Board. I was on the phone straight away to my parents. I couldn't believe it, then reality set in and I thought 'What do I do now?

Michael Bevan was also picked. He was back in the team after being dumped in the middle of the last summer. He was pretty excited, and we had a big night before heading for Adelaide.

When we arrived, I noticed a whole new culture. It was just the little things that made everything seem more professional. I got to my hotel room and my gear was already there. Training was really organised and everything we did was fully planned. It was a little bit daunting at first, but everyone made me feel welcome. Bob Simpson was still coach at that time. He was very encouraging and helpful. He took me aside and told me that my role in the side was to bowl 10 overs and score quick runs at the death. That seemed obvious, but it was good to be told because it helped me to settle down and made it easier to slide in. I was lucky to come in at a time when everything was going well.

But I did have a problem. I had some sort of virus and was struggling so much at training that I told the team physio, Errol Alcott. He gave me

some tablets and said, 'Well you've got to let Tubby [Mark Taylor] know.'
But I replied, 'No way! I'm not going to miss this opportunity to play.' So
I went into the game feeling crook.

I'm glad we batted first. I was excited and proud but really nervous
when I walked out. The ground seemed so small because I was used to
playing in front of next to no-one at Sheffield Shield matches, then all of a
sudden I was in the middle in front of a packed house with the crowd right
on top of me. I could hear individual voices. It was a strange feeling.

Luckily I was batting with Bevo, and once I got off the mark I didn't
feel so shaky. We put on 63 in 7 overs, and I thought I was on my way. I
was hitting the ball really well, and was beginning to relax. I was over the
moon, but a few games later I was out of the picture and back struggling for
New South Wales. Looking back, I know I wasn't ready for it. I was really
nervous for those first few games, and there was a lot of self-doubt. It wasn't
until I was 25 that I realised playing for Australia was what I really
wanted to do.

Four years later, few debuts in history could match Brett's cyclonic
arrival on the international stage. It was at the Melbourne Cricket
Ground, 28 December 1999, on the third day of the Second Test
against India. After making his initial steps on the elite arena as a
number 10 batsman, scoring 27, he proceeded to rip the Indians
apart with the ball.

It took just four deliveries for 'Binga' — his nickname comes
from the Bing Lee electrical goods chain — to justify the enormous
hype surrounding his selection. Left-handed opener Sadagopan
Ramesh was the stunned victim, beaten for pace and able only to
clip the ball with the inside edge of his bat before hearing the death
rattle and seeing Lee charging towards the slips cordon, almost
knocking Justin Langer to the ground with a hot-blooded run more
commonly seen at the MCG in the depths of winter. Brett Lee had
arrived in Test cricket. And Brett Lee belonged in Test cricket.

With his fastest delivery clocked by the Channel Nine speed
gun at 154.1 kilometres an hour, he became the thirteenth post-

war Australian to take five wickets on debut, claiming 5–47. He took two further wickets in the second innings for a match return of 7–78, his performance igniting hopes that Australia had welcomed the type of speed assassin not seen since Jeff Thomson nudged the 100-mile-an-hour barrier in the 1970s.

Brett laughs and says:

In my first over my only plan was to land the ball on the pitch. I was anxious, but I thought, 'Geez I'm not going to stuff this up now.' Luckily the first couple of balls were OK, and the crowd was right behind me. Then for the fourth ball, I ran in with the same plan — 'Just land it on the pitch Binga' — and the rest happened so quickly. I watched the ball hit the stumps, and I jumped, then started running like a madman. I know Langs copped a bit of a shoulder. It was a huge feeling. I couldn't believe it was happening. All the guys said, 'Watch the replay, watch the replay.' So I looked at it on the big screen over and over again. But I still couldn't believe it. That was the biggest wicket I've ever taken.

Batting before bowling in that match really helped me. It calmed my nerves. We'd lost a few wickets and I had to get my pads on. As I was dressing, I saw my name on the television scorecard at No. 10. I had to look twice because I was so used to seeing McDermott, McGrath, Kasprowicz, Fleming, Angel, anyone but me. For a moment I thought I was a spectator, then I realised, 'Shit I'm playing in this! This is it.'

I always put my left pad on first — it's nothing superstitious, it's just a routine. I did some stretches, checked my pads were on, and I must have checked my thigh pad six or seven times.

We lost another wicket, and Damien Fleming went out to join Shane Warne. I was in next. It didn't seem real. I sat next to Steve Waugh behind the huge windows upstairs in the dressing room. He told me, 'Binga, keep doing what you've been doing in the nets the last couple of days. You've been batting well.' He was so positive. I wasn't nervous, I was just anxious to get out there. Then Warney tried to clip one down leg-side off Ajit Agarkar and was caught by the keeper. All I could think was 'Don't give him out, please don't give him out.' But the finger went up, and I put on my green helmet — the first time I'd worn it was during practice when I was twelfth man in Perth a fortnight earlier. Back then it felt as though I couldn't have been hurt even if a truck had slammed into me — but this was different. This was the real thing.

As I walked out of the dressing room towards the players' gate, I felt my heart pumping really hard. I didn't want to, but I couldn't help looking at the big screen. All I saw was: Brett Lee 0, Runs 0, Average 0. I thought, 'Please don't nick the first ball, please let me get off the mark.'

The closer I got to the middle, the more I told myself to be positive and just watch the ball. I let the first ball go, which was a great relief because I reckon it would have cleaned me up if it had been on the stumps. I couldn't get off the mark for a couple of overs, but Flem was really helping me out, saying, 'Keep going, you're doing great.' Finally Javagal Srinath bowled a full toss outside off-stump and I went to drive the ball through the covers, but it slid through point for four. After that I was OK, and I knew I'd be right to bowl.

Shane was in the Members' Stand with two mates watching Brett's debut. He boasts he was one of the first people among the crowd of 23 127 to leap out of his seat when Ramesh's wicket was shattered. It was only a few years earlier that Brett, as a 19-year-old watching Australia play the West Indies on television, was bouncing on the sofa of the Lee family household, cheering his brother's opening international boundary, a clip off the toes against Courtney Walsh.

Each debut was an unforgettable day for the Lee boys. However, their careers had begun long before nervous steps were taken at the Adelaide Oval and the MCG. A pockmarked garage rollerdoor at the end of a sloping concrete driveway is proof that their cricketing heritage comes from the days when Shane, Brett and youngest brother Grant played the toughest of 'Test' matches in Mount Warrigal.

CHAPTER TWO

THE RATS OF OAK FLATS

When the boys were playing in the backyard, I couldn't even go and hang the washing out. I'd put the washing out, then the boys would decide they wanted to go out and have a game of cricket. They'd either take the wet washing off the line and just dump it somewhere, or they'd collapse the line with all the washing still on it. It would be nothing for me to hang the clothes out three or four times in a day. I gave up in the end, and never did any washing on the weekends when the boys were home.

Helen Lee

Mount Warrigal is situated on the back step of the steel city of Wollongong and is little more than an hour's drive south of Sydney. Despite its proximity to the city, it exudes a peaceful blend of coastal and rural charm. The waters of Lake Illawarra lap at the edges of suburbia and are bounded by gentle hills and rocky escarpments. Streets named after some of Australia's many memorable athletes and achievers: Konrads, Flak, Goolagong, Madigan, Gathercole, Lawrence and Winter, give the town a distinct sporting flavour. It's here in this pocket of memories that

Helen and Bob Lee raised their three boys to the beat of half-taped tennis balls thumping into their garage door.

Bob recalls:

They used to set the stumps up in front of the rollerdoor on the driveway beside the house. And the door would always be banging away. Bang, bang, bang. That's the second rollerdoor up there now. The first is under the house somewhere. It copped a real hammering. The boys used to open the gates and start their run-ups on the opposite side of the street, and they'd come charging in. We used to have a paling fence, and they used to hammer it too. That's probably why it fell down. They also played in the backyard. They'd stick their foam bodyboards up against the house windows to protect the glass. I can't believe we didn't have more broken windows. The garage window was broken one day, but that wasn't through playing cricket. That was a basketball.

There was no definitive moment when the Lees first took to cricket, but perhaps the early seeds were sown when Bob was a schoolboy in Cairns, in Far North Queensland. When just 11 years old, he was one of many wide-eyed youngsters holding their breaths as they watched West Indian fast bowler Wes Hall perform on their school oval.

Bob says:

He was enormous. We couldn't take our eyes off him. He was in town to promote cricket and he sure put on a show. He just rolled into bowl and broke two stumps. Just like that. It's amazing to think all these years later we're watching Brett bowl just as fast. Somebody, somewhere was pulling a few strings that day.

Hall, who was playing the 1961–62 Sheffield Shield season for Queensland, had previously been a central character in one of cricket's most entertaining and unforgettable Test series when Australia beat their Caribbean visitors 2–1 in a five-match campaign which included the first-ever tied Test. Hall, who took 21 wickets in the series, was a crowd favourite. His run-up accelerated all the way to the crease; he was strong, quick, and hostile. An intimidating sight.

Nowadays, there are few more exciting sights in world cricket than Brett sliding into the crease and firing bullets at batsmen who are forced to jump and hurry their shots. However, as Shane recalls, such speed didn't always dominate in the Mount Warrigal driveway cricket matches:

Brett was normally the bowler, Grant the fielder, and I batted. I was a big-time cheat back then. If I nicked the ball, I'd bluntly lie to Brett that I didn't hit it, and he'd whinge to Mum who'd have to come out and play the third umpire. She'd ask me, and I'd tell her I didn't hit it, so most of the time Brett just had to go back and bowl again. The only shots you could play were straight or a flick off the legs for four to the back fence. I'd get some more runs, then give Brett a bat, but I'd knock him over in a couple of balls, and he'd cry to Mum. Sometimes we'd sneak a proper six-stitcher into play, and believe it or not Brett used to be really scared of it. He'd put about four thigh pads on and he'd come out to bat looking like the Michelin Man.

We also kept really detailed statistics. We started writing them down on bits of paper, and then we eventually got a Commodore 64 computer which allowed us to work out a program for ratings. I was obviously rated number one because I was the oldest. I was also the captain, coach, umpire and scorer, so I did quite well. I averaged over 50, thanks to a fair bit of cheating. I was the biggest cheat in the world, but I was the oldest, so I had to be!

It's a funny thing that the three of us took to cricket like we did because Dad never played.

During his youth Bob Lee travelled a lot, never settling in the one town or city for too long. His father, William, a wharfie, was forced to leave Cairns with his wife and three sons when Bob was 13. The hunt for work took them on the road for five years, during which they spent time in Geelong and Newcastle, before settling in Wollongong. By this stage, after going through four different schooling systems, Bob earnt a scholarship to teachers' college, but he instead chose a career at the BHP steelworks. Thirty-two years later, he is still there as a qualified metallurgist.

Work opportunities also forced Milton Buxton, a builder, away from his home in the Hunter Valley of New South Wales. Milton and his family left Maitland and didn't settle again until, like the Lees, they arrived in Wollongong. Milton's daughter Helen was just five years old.

Seventeen years later the builder's daughter and wharfie's son met during the weekly Wednesday night dance at the 'Gong's local RSL Club. They were engaged within 12 months, and married soon afterwards on 17 June 1972. Shane was their first son, born in Wollongong Hospital on 8 August 1973; Brett followed on 8 November 1976, and then Grant — the last gift for the Lee family — on 20 November 1978.

Soccer, basketball, and skiing in the Snowy Mountains were three of the early sports the boys were introduced to during school holidays. On the rare times they were indoors, they were encouraged to play the piano.

Helen says:

They were all good, but Shane and Brett were too restless to take to the piano for long. Especially Brett. He was very good, but he didn't have time to learn because he couldn't sit still for five minutes. But he always loved his cricket. All the boys did. Shane started it. He was nine years old when he came home from school one day and first said he wanted to play in the local South Coast competition because all his friends were playing. I asked him: 'Why do you want to play that? It's so boring.' I had two brothers, and whenever we played cricket as children I was always out chasing the ball. It wasn't much fun to me. So, I talked Shane out of playing the first year, but the next year he said, 'No way, I'm going to join up.' And that was that.

The local club was Oak Flats, but the registrations had already closed, so Shane had his first season at Albion Park, a few kilometres away. He then came back to Oak Flats the following year.

Brett was only eight when he wanted to play, and because of his age he had to join Kanga Cricket, which used a soft ball. He didn't want to; all he wanted to do was play proper cricket like Shane. He had one season of Kanga Cricket, then moved up to the real thing. It was always funny watching him because he'd be all over the field. He'd bowl the ball, and no matter where it was hit he'd chase it as well. He should have been put on a leash.

By the time Grant began playing, all our Saturdays were devoted to cricket. We loved it. The boys were all in different teams, and with Bob's shift work it was always hard to spread ourselves between the matches, but we always tried to have at least someone with the boys while they were playing. I'd go with one, Bob would go with another, and Bob's parents were always there to take the third. It was important to always have someone there watching them.

All three boys showed instant talent. One match in particular reflected the skills that would one day be shown on the international arena: It was a windy day at Kiama, a town further south along the coast. Brett, playing for the Oak Flats Rats, was at the top of his mark preparing for his first game since graduating from Kanga Cricket. He was only nine years old, but already had a lust for fast bowling, which the Kiama batsmen soon learnt to fear. Helen remembers the day clearly:

Bob and I were both there. Brett had a big, long run-up, and as he went tearing in, his face would turn bright red, and his white blond hair would just flow behind him. First ball he comes in and bowls this boy, then the next one comes in and he bowls him too. The batsmen were all sharing pads, and they couldn't change them quickly enough. Some of the boys started crying, and I was getting a little embarrassed because as soon as they got their pads on, they were taking them off again. Brett took 6–0 in

the one over. All bowled. I was happy for him, but felt so sorry for the
other boys.

Brett's view of the day is short and simple: 'I just kept coming in and bowling full tosses and yorkers and the batsmen kept missing them. I thought, "Geez, how good is this game?" Ever since then, I've always wanted to bowl quickly.'

In a game against Gerringong during the same season, Oak Flats coach Graeme Creighton knew he was watching someone out of the ordinary:

When Brett started bowling, some of Gerringong's parents complained, saying Brett was just too fast, and his presence made it unfair. But I just had a quiet word to the parents, telling them to watch what Brett did. He always bowled right at the stumps. I told them there was no way in the world that I was going to harness someone who might be something special. It's hard to believe this was only Under-10s.

In those younger age groups, concentration is always the biggest problem, but Brett always had it. He knew what was going on, where the ball was going, and how to work out batsmen. He was ahead of his age. Even now I use him as a benchmark against other kids coming through.

And, as Bob Lee recalls, occasionally the kids coming through suffered:

There was a time when Brett was about 12 when there was just a normal training session going on at Oak Flats, and there was a new boy who'd come from another club. The supervisor sends him in all padded up. Brett comes in, bowls a bouncer at him with a proper cricket ball, and hits this kid in the mouth and knocks some teeth out. He had no helmet. I rang up his parents that night and offered to pay for all the dental work, but they were really nice about it and accepted it as something that happens. Brett was really upset about it, but I kept telling him it wasn't his fault.

This was Brett's first experience of another side of speed. He loved seeing batsmen backing away and stumps flying — a common sight against his bowling at this age — but he wasn't prepared for the other damage a cricket ball could do:

His name was Wesley Croft. When I bowled the first ball to him, I thought he looked quite good; then the next ball I sniffed him, and I remember hearing this really loud crack and I saw him stumbling. There was blood all over the pitch. I felt sick; it shocked me. As much as I wanted to bowl as fast as I could at that age, seeing the results made me think I'd gone too far.

Brett wasn't the only Lee boy feared for his pace. At first, Shane too was regarded as a tearaway. With a strong slinging action, his front foot rearing to near shoulder-height in his delivery stride, he was a difficult proposition on the bouncy concrete and synthetic wickets throughout the South Coast. By the time he graduated to turf pitches for Under-16 representative games, his reputation was widespread.

Jamie Annetts, one of Shane's former junior team-mates remembers:

We had an Under-17 Southern Zone selection trial in Nowra, and Shane never even had to turn up. He was at the Illawarra Academy of Sport back then, and there was all this talk about this Lee bloke. He was only 14 at the time. He was picked in the team, and I met him a fortnight later when Southern Zone played a trial game against Illawarra. I was wicket-keeper. When we went out to bowl, I was told by my coach to stand back a bit, and just as well I did because Shane started bowling thunderbolts. He scared the daylights out of the batsmen. I'd never kept to anyone faster. In the country, word spreads pretty quickly about good players, and I did my part by going back to my home town of Goulburn and telling all the senior players: 'Ooh geez I've just been playing juniors with this bloke and you'd want to watch out if you play him because he bowls bloody bullets.' He was quick all right.

Such praise was common for the three Lee boys, who all walked a well-worn path through the representative ranks. As students of Balarang Primary — just a 10-minute walk from home — Brett, then Grant, followed Shane's lead by earning State schoolboy selection.

Shane recalls:

They were the first major teams any of us got picked for. The year I made it, the Australian championships were in Adelaide. That seemed a world away. I was so excited because the team flew down, and I'd never been on a plane before. It was my very first cricket tour at 11 years of age. I'll never forget it. The family drove all the way to see me play.

State representation continued when the boys progressed to Oak Flats High with their inevitable selection into the NSW Combined High Schools teams. Throughout those early years, the boys sprinted ahead of their age groups, graduating to the South Coast Men's Competition long before their junior commitments were over. Shane remembers he played his first senior game when he was still in the Under-12s:

Mum and Dad were really worried, but they let me have a go. It was fourth grade, and the bowlers turned out to be just too fast, and I was too little. I didn't play grade for another two years after that, but by then I was OK, and after starting off in third grade, I made it to first grade within a couple of games as an opening bowler.

Brett recalls little about his introduction to the senior ranks as a 13-year-old:

I think we played against Shellharbour. It felt really different because the guys seemed so much older than me. Most of them were about 25 to 30, and I was still a junior at school. It was such a big difference. I bowled first change at first; I think I picked up two wickets, and I progressed from there. It was a really steady start, but I always knew I had a real chance of making it. At that stage I was really scared of the ball. Growing up I was always worried about copping some bad hits, getting bounced out or getting hurt. It was quite intimidating at first, going out at number 11 and facing grown men. I felt I didn't belong there, but there was no way I was going to stop.

Of all the early childhood memories, the games when Shane and Brett played in a team together were among the most significant moments.

Brett says:

Our first game together was for Oak Flats High. My earliest memory is when we beat a touring English team from Petersborough Schools. Shane was captain. He smashed 106, and I took a couple of wickets. They were my first international scalps! We were both over the moon. Shane was just about to finish school, and I was just about to start. It was great that we had the chance.

Apart from school cricket and the South Coast Competition, the boys' development was helped by the Illawarra Academy of Sport in Wollongong. Shane was selected for the first intake of players for the Academy's part-time cricket program in 1988. Thirteen-year-old Brett followed the next year, and stayed for another two years.

Bruce Jones, former coaching co-ordinator, says:

I have some very good memories, especially with Shane when the Academy team first toured New Zealand. We played against regional development squads, and whenever we got into trouble Shane always seemed to come in and save us with either bat or ball. Although he was better known in the South Coast for his bowling, we knew he was going to be a genuine all-rounder. We knew he could bowl, but he could bat better. He had talent from the word go.

Brett was the same. I remember putting a call through to Alan Campbell, the junior coaching boss of New South Wales Cricket, and saying: 'Hey, we've got a 13-year-old down here who I think you better keep your eye on.' Two years later the Academy played a game in Wollongong against the Canterbury Under-17 team from New Zealand. Canterbury had this huge opener who was about 6 foot 4 and 14 stone. Brett soon put him on his backside when he let one go, and the opener came off saying, 'He's just too quick for us. Just too quick.'

Comments like that confirmed what we already knew. You can pick up special qualities in players. And it's not only obvious talent. It's the other things they do, like the boy who does that little bit extra. He just doesn't wait to be told what to do when training is on. I can remember watching and being impressed by Brett bowling to his dad before training. He was so keen to play, but just as importantly, he was so keen to learn. And so was his Dad. Bob didn't have a great depth of coaching knowledge in those early days, but he was great to have as a back-up. He would listen to what you were trying to tell them, then he'd go away and work on that with either Brett or Shane, or both of them.

Despite his lack of intricate knowledge about cricket coaching, Bob Lee gave his sons every opportunity to develop their games, and in doing so he showed that the Lee family had a special bond, which was widely recognised throughout the community. Bob and the boys were a familiar sight in the nets opposite Balarang Primary, where they trained after school. Nestled in the corner of Panorama Oval, the nets received the same punishment a particular rollerdoor did.

Shane remembers:

Yeh, they copped a caning. We used to go down religiously every afternoon. We'd all be waiting for Dad to come home from work, then away we'd go. Sometimes our Uncle Les would come down too. He'd bowl off-spin and my old man used to try to bowl quick. As we all got older, and it was recognised that Brett, Grant and I all had some potential, Mum and Dad were just so supportive. They never pushed us, but were always there for us. Uncles, aunties, grandparents too; they were all very loving. Dad was a real classic. We used to call him 'the doctor' because he seemed to know everything. He used to wear a pair of really worn-out stubbies and thongs, but he always made sure we had the good cricket gear, clothes, and schoolbooks. We always came first.

Brett and I obviously owe a lot to our cricket coaches throughout the years, but we'd be nowhere without 'the doctor' and Mum. From the time I was born, they'd never had a holiday alone until I shouted them one a few years ago to Hamilton Island. It's good to give something back because they gave up so much for us. In 1999, Dad had this real bomb of a car that wouldn't get through rego, so Brett and I chipped in and bought 'the doctor' a ute.

Mum and Dad basically lived their lives for us. They still do, and they'd be exactly the same if we were still playing for the Oak Flats Rats.

Or in the backyard.

CHAPTER THREE

SHANE MAKES THE GRADE

*Proved himself a wicket-taking fast bowler in his
first season, despite our catching efforts. With the
change over period behind him, Shane will improve
rapidly next season. His fielding is excellent and we
know the batting ability is there. At his age, we all look
forward to a long and very successful career.*
Campbelltown Cricket Club Year Book, 1990–91

At the Lee family household, there is a shoebox covered in pictures of
teddy bears that is tucked carefully away in the living room.
Continually fattened by Helen adding new handfuls of memorabilia,
it is as valuable as any silverware or family jewels. It bursts with
pennants, yellowing newspaper articles, representative badges, school
reports, and anything else that tells of the achievements of Shane, Brett
and Grant. The story from these precious records makes it obvious
that Shane was not only an all-rounder in cricket, but off the field as
well. There are cards from his primary school teachers, rewarding his
'excellent' work in mathematics, reading and writing. There are also
Oak Flats High awards for basketball and athletics in which Shane was
twice named the school's Age Champion. He recalls:

Sport was something I was always good at, but when I was growing up I never considered it as a career. I was quite studious at school, and never had to be asked to do my homework. Dad was really big on that; he always stressed success at school was very important, but the older I became the more cricket played a more important role. Whenever I did well at school or in the local competition, I couldn't wait until the following Wednesday morning to see if my name was mentioned in the local paper, the Lake Times. *By Year 8, I'd made the NSW Combined High Schools Second XI, and was picked in the firsts every year after that. It cost Mum and Dad hundreds of dollars because I was always bringing home catalogues with the latest gear to buy. At that age it was cool to be able to walk around school with a representative tracksuit top on!*

You didn't have to look that hard to realise I was a big cricket fan. In Year 10, I had pictures of Steve Waugh and Dean Jones from the 1989 Ashes tour on some of my folders. Looking back, it's weird to think that I idolised those guys and put them on a pedestal that was out of reach. And then within a few years I was playing with and against them.

Shane's success at school level cricket was mirrored by his achievements in local representative teams, which led to interest from Sydney grade clubs Saint George and Campbelltown. At first, Bob and Helen Lee thought their son would be best off going to Saint George, a club that boasted the rich tradition of grooming players such as Don Bradman, Norm O'Neill, and Brian Booth. However, the efforts made by Campbelltown officials swayed the Lees towards the club in Sydney's south-west. President Noel Lamming and first grade captain Mark England drove to Mount Warrigal to take the Lees to dinner and discuss Shane's future. By the end of the evening, it was agreed Shane would play for Campbelltown in the Under-16 Green Shield Competition in the 1988–89 season.

It was a successful start to his Sydney career. He played nine games for a return of 300 runs at an average of 42.86, and 19 wickets at 10.95. During the same season, he gained the attention of NSW Cricket officials when he was named 'Bowler of the Week' at the state's coaching class for country players.

The following season, Shane leapt further into the selectors' books as a player of the future when he was picked in the Australian Under-17 squad after impressive performances for the NSW team, which finished third at the national championships in Adelaide. His best game was against South Australia when he blasted 102 and took 4–55. The 16-member national squad spent a week in Adelaide training at the Cricket Academy, during which time Shane enhanced his reputation as an aggressive bowling all-rounder in front of the then head coach, Jack Potter.

But such aggression wasn't limited to cricket. Bob Lee recalls an incident at Mount Warrigal that tells much about Shane's sense of competition:

Shane was 16 at the time. We were playing basketball in the driveway when he drove past me, caught my finger and pulled it back. I was in a lot of pain, so the game basically finished there and then. The next day he wanted to have a bit of a spar with me in the lounge room. At that age he always wanted to beat me at everything. My finger was still very sore, so I put one hand in my pocket and just sparred with the other hand, keeping it open so I wouldn't hurt him. Then all of a sudden he launched one at me with a bloody fist! He knocked me on the jaw and sent me back about 3 feet, then he raced out the back yelling. I was going to kill him, but I couldn't catch him. He raced down the road and kept bloody going. He'd have the confidence to stand his ground these days.

More heavyweight contests would come in 1990–91 when Shane was chosen in Campbelltown's first grade team. He was just 17, and still at school. Shane remembers:

Until I got my P-plates, Mum or Dad used to drive me to training twice a week. It took about an hour each way, and then we drove all over Sydney clocking up hundreds of kilometres for games on the weekend. They were every Saturday, and most Sundays because at that stage I was still eligible for the Poidevin-Gray Under-21 competition.

First-grade was a nerve-racking experience. Campbelltown had a slick side with a really good batting line-up including Michael Bevan and Martin Haywood, two class-spinners, Mark England and Tom Shiner, and a pretty frightening pace-attack led by West Indian left-armer Ken McLeod. I was first-change bowler and batted 9.

I remember my first game was at North Sydney Oval. McLeod was bowling really fast, forcing the keeper to stand the furthest back I'd ever seen a keeper stand. There was a nick off just the third ball of the match, and the second slip took the catch diving forward. It was a screamer, and all I could think was, 'Geez how good are these guys? They're too good for me. I'm out of my depth big time.' I was shitting myself, it was the most nervous I'd ever been.

But I was lucky enough to have a fair game, taking two wickets. Trevor Chappell was my first. I bowled him with a yorker. It was the first ball of my second spell, and I ended up being on a hat-trick, but missed out. I didn't do as well batting. I'd only got a couple before Chappell got his revenge when he had me out hooking.

Shane finished the season with 23 wickets at 31.48, and 165 runs at 16.5 from 15 matches. His march towards higher honours continued over the next two seasons. In 1991–92, he took 31 wickets at 23.5, finishing second behind McLeod with 35 wickets. His batting was less rewarding, yielding just 106 runs in 10 matches, and prompting this assessment in Campbelltown's *Year Book*:

Whether he was bowling with the new or old ball, Shane showed he has the persistence, variation and control to take wickets. Apart from a sparkling 48 against Gordon, he would admit his batting was disappointing. By improving his consistency in this area, Shane has the potential to become one of the most respected all-rounders in grade cricket.

Despite his poor return with the bat, his innings against Gordon was noticed by some significant judges. NSW batsman Mark O'Neill and wicket-keeper Phil Emery watched their rival from close quarters. Emery remembers:

Shane would have been batting 8 or 9. He hit the ball really pure, and played everything well with lots of time. At one stage Mark O'Neill, who was one of the best judges of a cricketer I knew, turned to me from first slip and said, 'This guy is easily the best bat they've got.' I asked Mark who the guy was, and he answered, 'I don't know, but I think he's their opening bowler.' It was obvious Shane had an enormous amount of talent.

That talent was recognised again by selectors when Shane was picked in the Australian Under-19 development squad after NSW finished runner-up to Western Australia at the national championships in Perth. Shane took 17 wickets for the carnival, including a haul of 7–77 against the ACT.

The squad included future Test players Ricky Ponting and Murray Goodwin (Zimbabwe); and Matthew Mott, Martin Love and Jimmy Maher, who were marking time before Sheffield Shield selection.

Shane too was closing in on the first-class scene, but at that stage he wasn't devoting all his time to cricket. After completing the Higher School Certificate in 1991, he began studies the following year at Wollongong University. The full-time commitments were to last only two years before cricket duties forced Shane to defer, and it wasn't until 2000 that he finally graduated with a Degree in Science, majoring in Psychology and Marketing.

Shane says:

It took a long time but I was determined to finish it. If I start something I always finish it, but it was hard going back over the last few years. I'd become a pretty poor student, and by the time I resumed after my deferment, I didn't go to many lectures because by then I'd moved to Sydney. But some of the classes I did go to were quite entertaining. Forget working out the subjects, I reckon most of the students were trying to work themselves out!

When I finally received the degree in the post, it was actually one of the biggest thrills of my life.

Shane's cricket graduation was to be much quicker than his stroll through the tertiary education ranks. By 1992–93 he'd moved into the New South Wales Sheffield Shield squad, and his mother was about to start another section in the shoebox.

CHAPTER FOUR

AWAKENING THE SLEEPING STAR

The first time I was twelfth man for New South Wales was at a Mercantile Mutual Cup game in Brisbane. There was talk leading up to the match that it was between Glenn McGrath and me for carrying the drinks. He was in his first season of State cricket too, and he got the nod to play ahead of me. I was rooming with Brad McNamara and although I was only twelfth man I was very conscious of doing the right thing. This was the closest I'd been to playing for the State. I was really nervous and went to bed early, then the phone rang about three in the morning, but whoever it was just hung up when I answered. It happened about another five or six times, so I threw the phone off the hook, but I forgot all about the wake-up call. The next thing I know there was a porter knocking on the door saying, 'Mark Taylor said you are late, and you better get your arses down to the ground straight away.' I woke Brad up, and we bolted down to the ground without a shower, hair everywhere, shirts inside out. When we arrived, the rest of the team were doing a

warm-up lap, and I thought, 'Christ I've had a shocker
here.' I tried to explain, but Tubby said, 'Don't bother.'
What a start!

Shane Lee

What an impression! Arriving late and dishevelled, Shane was understandably worried that his interstate cricket career had run its distance before it had even started. However, his late arrival at the Gabba certainly didn't affect his team's performance. Led with a brilliant 131 by Steve Waugh, NSW defeated Queensland by 11 runs. Nearly three months later, on 31 January 1993, Shane finally made his State debut in a Mercantile Mutual Cup game against Tasmania at the Sydney Cricket Ground. In a nervous start with the new ball he took 1–44 off 8 overs, his only wicket coming when he bowled Jamie Cox for 8. Batting at number 10, he was 4 not out after hitting a boundary down the ground to give his side a two-wicket victory. Shane remembers:

I was only 19, but wasn't as nervous as I thought I'd be. I'd already played a few NSW Second XI games that season, and apart from the match in Brisbane, I'd been twelfth man in a couple of Sheffield Shield games, including the one that had finished only the day before against Tasmania. I already felt I was a small part of the team, and there was a huge amount of pride and winning arrogance among the players. The Waughs were involved in the Fifth Test against the West Indies in Perth, and Mike Whitney was also out of the team. So we weren't at full strength, but the players who came in knew what was expected of them; everyone was heading in the one direction.

Much of that credit had to be given to Steve Rixon, who was a hard coach. I never really knew what he was thinking, but he always seemed to know what I was thinking. He was the only coach I'd ever had with that sixth sense.

Apart from the Tasmania game being my debut it was a pretty insignificant match for me, but at least my career was underway. As much as anything I remember being given my playing gear, and I was so rapt that I went home, put the blue pants and shirt on, and walked around the house all night in them.

A bigger moment came just a couple of days later when I was chosen in the Sheffield Shield team to play Western Australia at the SCG. This time I was nervous, very nervous. The whole game I was worried about what everyone was thinking, what the players were thinking, the crowd, the journalists, and my family. I never walked onto the ground thinking I'd do well. Although I'd been consistent in grade, I looked at the Shield as a completely different ball game.

Geoff Marsh won the toss and decided to bat. That meant I was into it straight away. I couldn't believe I was getting the new ball. Sure I'd got it a few days earlier in the Mercantile Mutual game, but this was different. This was first-class cricket.

When I was at the top of my mark, I felt myself shaking. It was unbelievable. The first few deliveries came out really rough; I was getting the ball to swing heaps, and I just couldn't control it. I ended up getting 1–66 off 15 overs, and my wicket ball was probably the worst ball I bowled. It was short and really wide; Geoff Marsh smashed it, and I thought 'Yeh, that's crap, that's four'. But then Trevor Bayliss in gully dived full length and caught it left-handed. I'd never seen a catch as good; I was so grateful to him.

I was just as shaky when I batted. I came in at number 9, and got off the mark with a nick through slips off Brendon Julian. Then off-spinner Steve Herzberg cleaned me up for 4.

I only bowled two overs in the second dig because our spinners Greg Matthews and David Freedman did all the work. Moey took eight wickets to shatter WA on the last day, and we ended up winning by seven wickets. It was a great win, but I honestly can't remember all that much about it. I was just too nervous. Once you're comfortable, you tend to take in more around you, but not for me in those early days.

However, in the absence of Mark Taylor, stand-in captain Phil Emery does recall some of the finer details:

At first Shane was really quiet, which wasn't surprising considering how young he was. He was just a boy. All year at training he was certainly excited to be there, but most of the time he just shut up, ran from the top of his mark, and put in.

In the match against WA, it was a pretty hot day, the track was flat and I knew we really had our work cut out against a strong team. I had Shane bowling uphill, and Wayne Holdsworth bowling down. Shane went for quite a few in his first few overs, so I gave him a break, but wanted to bring him back downhill after Wayne had bowled his first spell. I called Shane up again, threw him the ball, and said, 'Right you're on.' He had this horrified look on his face as if to say, 'Oh shit here we go!' He was really nervous because all he could say was: 'You don't expect me to bowl again do you?' I replied, 'Well you are our opening bowler, and I'm not going to do it!' It was one of the few times he'd been shy in his life, but thankfully he bowled better and gained a bit of confidence after Trevor Bayliss took the screamer.

The other thing I remember about Shane from that match didn't happen until after we'd finished. He was in the dressing room quietly packing his bag, and was about to leave when I asked, 'Where are you going?' He just said a little surprised, 'Game's over, I'm going home.' But I shook my head: 'No mate, it's not over yet. It's a good win, my first as captain, it's time to celebrate.' So we had a few beers, and after a while it was the most at ease I'd seen him all season.'

It was Shane's last appearance in the dressing room for the season. While New South Wales finished strongly to win the Sheffield Shield and Mercantile Mutual Cup, Shane returned to the Australian Under-19 squad for a 10-match tour of New Zealand. His best performance came in the first of two Tests against the New Zealand youth team when he took eight wickets for the match and scored 51 in the second innings. The game was a draw, but Australia went on to lose the series after being outplayed in the Second Test.

At this stage of his career Shane was beginning to emerge as a true all-rounder, not just an opening bowler who could bat a bit.

For the first time his batting overshadowed his bowling in Sydney grade. He finished the season with 360 runs at 40, and 16 wickets at 28.2. And his dominance of those his own age was highlighted by his Poidevin-Gray statistics: 4 matches, 3 not outs, 318 runs, 146 highest score (not out), 318 average; 42 overs, 9 wickets, 8.1 average. The recognition of his potential was continuing to grow.

He is undoubtedly the best all-round prospect in NSW, if not Australia. If he has the desire to hone his game to perfection and develop Dennis Lillee like dedication to bowling fitness, the cricket world is at his feet. (*Campbelltown Year Book*, 1992–93)

Despite his graduation to the first-class ranks, there was still a strong sense of youthful innocence about his performances. This was no better illustrated than at a training session when Mike Whitney jokingly labelled the new all-rounder 'Garfield', in reference to the great West Indian Sir Garfield Sobers. Shane's reply was as refreshing as it was naive: 'What do you mean? I look nothing like a big orange cat!'

'Ug' became a longer-lasting nickname, an obvious play on words with his surname — 'Ug-Lee'. However, 'Kilometres' would have been just as suitable because Shane was still living at home and driving to Sydney as many as four times a week. Helen Lee recalls it was a hard existence:

He had State training twice a week, and matches and functions to attend. All that on top of the study he was still doing. He used to come home very tired, but he never complained because he knew he just had to do it. He didn't have the money to move to Sydney, so it was a case of making the best out of the situation that he could.

Shane was soon to sample life away from home as a tier-scholarship member of the Australian Cricket Academy in Adelaide. The letter of confirmation from head coach Rod Marsh summed up in one very simple sentence what was expected: 'You have been offered the scholarship at the Academy because there are enough people in the right places who believe you could play for Australia.'

During the '93 winter Shane made several trips to the Academy and the Institute of Sport in Canberra. The kilometres continued clicking over in 1993–94. And so did the opportunities. Shane was overlooked for the first part of the NSW season, managing only a brief appearance as twelfth man in the Sheffield Shield match against Western Australia in Perth. It was an eleventh-hour call-up when the late withdrawal of Greg Matthews, who was recovering in hospital following an incident at a Perth nightclub, forced the team to make changes. Despite his limited role, Shane still left a mark on the game, throwing down the stumps from mid-off to dismiss Geoff Marsh for 128 in WA's only innings. It proved to be a miserable game for the Blues. They lost in two days, prompting Sydney's *Daily Telegraph* to run a back-page spread of the players and their scores unkindly etched on tombstones. It was an image that motivated the team for the rest of the season.

The return match against WA in February signalled Shane's return and a change of fortunes for NSW. Inspired by an unbeaten 203 from Michael Bevan, the home team won by nine wickets. Shane scored 7 in his only chance with the bat, but his single-wicket hauls in each innings were significant because Geoff Marsh was the victim on both occasions. When added to the run-out earlier in the season, and Shane's initial Shield wicket the previous year, Marsh had become a Lee bunny!

The next outing against South Australia at the SCG had a telling influence on the rest of Shane's season. After a discussion with selector Neil Marks, captain Phil Emery promoted his youngest player to number 5 in the Blues' order. Shane scored 17 in his only chance at the crease before falling to leg-spinner Peter McIntyre. NSW won by an innings and 70 runs, and Emery had seen enough to retain Shane in the same position for the following match in

Sydney against Queensland. Sent in to bat, the Blues finished the opening day at 5–284, with Shane unbeaten on 38 and on the verge of the biggest moment in his brief career to date. He recalls:

Towards the end of the first day, David Freedman came in as nightwatchman. We had about 12 overs to face, Carl Rackemann was bowling really quickly, and I just went into survival mode, fending balls off and popping them just out of the reach of fieldsmen. But that wasn't my natural game, so I took a punt and decided to have a go, and was lucky enough to hook and pull a few boundaries before stumps.

The next day was really hot, and the wicket had really flattened out. I got off to a flier and the next thing I knew I was on about 60, and it was only then that I thought to myself, 'Geez I'm a chance of a hundred here.' I tried to stay positive, and by the time I was into the nineties Stuart Law came on to bowl his part-time leggies. There was a bit of relief when I saw him come to the crease, but it made me concentrate harder. Luckily he bowled me a couple of long hops, I put them away, and got to 100 without having any time to be nervous. I looked up at the scoreboard, saw the three figures, and got really excited. It was total elation, I was sweating as much as I think I've ever sweated, and my heart was pounding like a sledgehammer. It was a great moment. My maiden first-class ton. The most important thing was that I'd proven myself at that level. We declared soon after, and I walked off 104 not out. When I got to the dressing room, Phil Emery said to me, 'Well batted mate, but I never thought you'd get a hundred!'

I couldn't stop thinking how funny it was the way things had worked out. Here I was taking the new ball in my first few matches, then all of a sudden I was scoring a century at number 5. It had evolved over two years, but really it was only four games. In those early Shield matches and one-dayers, I was always more confident with my batting than bowling. I knew I could do it, and was disappointed when I was batting so low. So when I got the chance to move up the order, I put a bit of pressure on myself because I really wanted it to work out. And it did, but I still wasn't a genuine all-rounder because my bowling wasn't quite right at that stage.

I started the second innings really confidently until Geoff Foley bowled a bouncer which got through my grill, smacked me on the cheek, and knocked me off my feet. I retired hurt for 17, but it didn't matter much because we went on to win the game by 51 runs, and a week later we were hosting the Shield Final against Tasmania. That match really proved you're only as good as your last innings because I got cleaned up by Shaun Young for a duck in my only bat, and I didn't get a wicket. But we won by an innings and 61 runs. Michael Bevan scored a hundred, and Brad McNamara had a great game, getting a century and four first-innings wickets before Phil Alley did the damage in the second dig with 'five-for'.

It was great to be part of that team, especially after we'd copped such a bagging earlier in the season for the two-day loss in Perth. Apart from the Test players who were away for much of the season, we didn't have too many outstanding players. Obviously Bevo was an exception, but the rest of us just did our jobs; everyone contributed at some stage of the season, and we all wanted to enjoy each other's success. Despite the Perth match, we never thought we were going to lose that year. We used to train hard, there was good discipline, and we were playing really good cricket. The feeling in the squad was just so confident.

Although I only played four games, I felt I'd had an important role. I was considered one of three all-rounders in the side, together with 'Buzzard' McNamara and Neil Maxwell. Normally you'd think we'd be vying for the one spot, but one night after training early in the season Maxey said, 'This is bullshit. We can all play in this team if we perform. And we can make it a winning team.' That's when the three of us began calling ourselves the 'engine room'. We normally batted 5, 6, and 7, and if the top order got knocked over early, then the 'engine room' would kick in and try to get the runs. We developed a real bond that ended up spreading further than the cricket field.

The trio also figured in the Blues' successful Mercantile Mutual Cup campaign, although Shane's contribution in the rain-interrupted final against Western Australia at the SCG was restricted to 4 runs and 1–18 from 3 overs. NSW won by 43 runs. Shane's most rewarding return came at home in the previous match against South Australia when he scored 44 off 55 balls and took 2–31 off 9 overs in a contest South Australia won on a revised run rate.

However, one of the most memorable moments of the season came in the fourth round of the Sydney grade competition at Campbelltown's Raby Oval. Opening the bowling, Shane took 5–86 against the University of New South Wales. And at the other end, a lithe 16-year-old tearaway took 4–58. In his first two-day game with the club, Brett had arrived with the same gusto that would later herald his entry into the Test arena. It was the brothers' first match together in three years and their performances left club officials in no doubt that the Waugh twins wouldn't be the only family combination to steal the headlines in the 1990s.

Shane's five-wicket haul was one of three in a grade season that yielded 36 scalps at 23.14 and 713 runs, including two centuries, at 71.3. His achievements were gaining considerable attention, prompting the media to gaze into the crystal ball:

> Within two years Australia will have Campbelltown's strapping Shane Lee in their World Series ranks. Barely 20, Lee is the pace bowler-batsman Australia needs.
>
> But, like Julian, Lee bowls too many wides at present. His strength is that he is a bowler who bats well, described by Australian Cricket Academy coach Rod Marsh as 'the hardest hitter I have ever seen'. (Phil Wilkins, *Sydney Morning Herald*, 24 January 1994)

Shane was given further opportunity to impress Marsh when he spent the '94 off-season as a full-time student of the Academy where, he recollects, he developed more than just his cricketing skills:

It was a good learning curve: living out of home I had to look after myself for the first time. We only received $60 a month, and all our food was supplied. Between training sessions I used to work at the South Australian Cricket Association in Administration. That gave me a few extra dollars.

I missed home a little bit, but because our whole days were taken up, except Sundays, time went pretty quickly. Most of the weeks were carefully scheduled. We trained twice a day, first a morning session which would generally be weights or aerobics, then afternoons were normally skills. It was a very competitive setup, not only in cricket, but in many things we did: who was the best at the vertical jump, the quickest runner, the strongest.

We also did a small business management course and public speaking, which were both great. The Academy was about life education as well.

Discipline was one of the best things I learnt: getting up early to train and work, and most importantly getting into a routine. That was a big plus. At the Academy they don't try to turn you into Test cricketers, but they try to prepare you a little bit quicker for the opportunities that you have to make happen. The whole perception of the Academy has changed since '94. At times there's been negative press about young guys going there thinking they'd automatically return to play for their states, then Australia. The bottom line is that it's still up to you, no matter what training you have or where you go.

My time there remains one of the best years of my life, and I came away with some very close mates. We all trained really hard for nine months, but we also had a good time as well. Rod Marsh was all for that. Train hard, then have a few beers at the weekend. But he was tough if we did the wrong thing. I remember one Saturday morning, just before we were going on a tour: Our last session was to be a weights workout. I'd been out on a huge night with fast bowler Simon Cook just a couple of nights before. But most of the other guys went out on the Friday, and when we got down to the weights room the next morning, Rod could smell the alcohol on everyone. He said, 'Right, everyone down to the beach now.'

For the next hour, we were doing sprints up to our waists in freezing water at Henley Beach. Some of the guys were throwing up and were doing it really tough, but Rod kept on pushing us. He taught us a lesson there.

I have a lot of respect for Rod because he's really honest, and always tells you what he thinks. He's very good to speak to about cricket, he's very *knowledgeable, and gets the desired results. I always tried hard to impress him and other influential people who came to talk to us, like Ian Chappell and Dennis Lillee. It was very important to perform in front of them; every player wanted to walk away from the Academy thinking they'd left an impression.*

Shane returned to NSW for 1994–95, a season that began with promise but ended in disappointment. Nine Shield matches yielded a respectable 434 runs at 28.93, but only 8 wickets at 68.8. In four Mercantile Mutual Cup games he scored 71 runs at 17.75 with a strike rate of 68.27, and he took 3 wickets at 36.67. The Blues finished second last in the Shield with just two wins, and they failed to trouble any side in the one-dayers. Shane says:

Coming back from the Academy I was looking forward to a really big season. Although the team started badly with a heavy loss against the Vics in Melbourne, I had a pretty good game, taking 3–53 and scoring 86 in the first innings. Two matches later, I was over the moon after hitting 100 not out against Tasmania in the day/night Shield at the SCG. Tassie had left-armer Chris Matthews, who was near the end of his career but could still send them through. Unfortunately Greg Matthews, who I was batting with for part of the innings, tried to fire Chris up by walking back to the mark and talking in his ear. Chris started bowling about 7 yards quicker and I thought, 'Moey, you idiot.' But I saw it through, and ended up bringing up the 100 with a six over long-on off Matthews. I felt great in the second innings too with 52 off 38 balls before I ran myself out. That was only three games into the season, and I thought I was on a roll, but I fell away badly from then on.

By the last Shield game of the season I was dropped to twelfth man. That was a great lesson for me. I knew it had been coming, and I got to the stage where I was actually relieved when it happened. Until then I was spending a lot of time worrying about my form, and that only made things worse. In my last five Shield innings I'd scored 45 runs, and not taken a wicket. It was then time to go into the off-season, get away from the game for a while, and have a think about how I could get my thoughts back in order. It was a tough time. I still considered myself a relatively new player on the scene, and I was always worrying about consistency. It affected me badly. Instead of just going out and playing, I was putting too much pressure on myself.

The feeling in the team also made it harder. It was the first season since I'd started that NSW were spending some long sessions in the field. We weren't bowling teams out at much as we used to, we were complacent, expecting things to happen without putting in the work.

It was the start of a lean and, at times, turbulent period for NSW. Steve Rixon resigned to take up the position of New Zealand's coach, leaving the way for former Test fast bowler Geoff Lawson to begin a new career in 1995–96. That season was also to launch Shane into the international spotlight.

CHAPTER FIVE

PAIN AND PACE

I really didn't like cricket until I became friends
with Brett. I didn't really understand it, but he was
always telling me things about the game, especially
why and how fast bowlers bowled certain deliveries.
He just had a real passion for the game. Cricket was
made for Brett. And Brett was made for cricket.

Adam Rainford

On their way home from school, Brett and his best mate Adam Rainford used to pass through a paddock just a block away from the Lee's home. Sometimes they stayed there for hours, chatting about their dreams while sitting on a hill that overlooked Oak Flats High. Brett's ambition was simple: 'I want to play cricket for Australia.' It wasn't an unusual wish — generations of Australian boys have had similar dreams. However, unlike the thousands of others who realise sooner or later that their best games are played in their sleep, Brett had an obvious trait that separated him from the masses ... TALENT. He also had a fierce self-belief:

It may seem weird, but somehow or other I always knew I was going to play for Australia. I was always wishing and hoping, and trying my best to get there. And deep down I knew that I could. That was from about the age of 10.

There was a time when I wanted to go all the way in basketball, but after a while I knew I was never going to make it. I was always a very small kid growing up.

But things started to change when I reached high school. I had these whopping size-13 feet in Year 7, and I slowly started growing into them. Then at about 14 I just shot up, and my bowling got a lot stronger and quicker. At the same time, Shane was starting to make a name for himself in Sydney grade cricket, and that helped motivate me. I was still only playing junior representative cricket, but I knew it was a stepping stone to following Shane.

Shane, Grant and I watched a lot of cricket on TV, and I kept imagining what it would be like to be in the middle of the SCG or MCG bowling flat out in front of a packed crowd. It really excited me. I idolised all the Australian players, but my favourite bowler was South Africa's Allan Donald. I remember watching him at the 1992 World Cup. I loved the way he used to steam in, bowl flat-chat, and make the batsmen hurry up. I thought he was great and wanted to be just like him. I never wanted to do anything in cricket other than bowl as fast as I could. I loved the thrill of it and the excitement of getting batsmen jumping round. Maybe I was young and naive, but I never doubted I could make it.

However, it wouldn't be easy. While the 1992–93 season was going to be a highlight of Shane's career, it would present Brett with a painful challenge he hadn't yet faced. The first serious injury of his life was about to test his character.

Injuries are like taxes. Both are impossible to avoid, and good management is needed to reduce their impact. At the Australian Under-17 Championships in Hobart in January 1993, Brett was too young to understand marginal rates or negative gearing, but he discovered how important it was to protect his assets, especially his right arm.

Brett remembers:

NSW had a camp in Hobart before the carnival and during a training session some of the players started having a throwing contest. It was a stupid thing to do because we were all trying to outdo each other, and were putting a lot of pressure on our arms. At the end, my arm felt quite sore, but I didn't worry about it.

I had no problems in the first few games, but in the semi-final against Queensland I chased a ball right to the boundary and was under pressure for a good throw because the batsmen were going back for a fourth run on a very big field. I tried to throw the ball as flat and hard as possible, but I put so much into it that my arm just snapped. It was a sickening noise that was so loud that even the people in the grandstand heard it. It was just like a twig snapping. I immediately had pins and needles, and the arm puffed up and was very red. The team officials put it in a sling, and I walked off thinking my arm was broken.

Mum and Dad, who were watching, took me straight to hospital for X-rays. The doctors told me I'd either snapped or torn a tendon, and I had to keep the arm in a sling for four weeks, but I never had to have plaster on it. After four weeks I started getting back into training again, but the arm was still really sore when I bowled and threw. I was just told to keep strengthening it and everything would be sweet.

I didn't play much cricket for the rest of the season and hoped that a good rest over the winter would make it better. But during that time, I often found it hard to sleep because my arm was aching so much that it was waking me up. After telling Mum, we just accepted it was taking a while to heal.

I played on during the next season, but midway through, about a year after I'd originally done the injury, I went and had another X-ray, and was told that I'd had a fracture there for 12 months. I put up the old X-ray taken in Hobart against the new X-rays, and they were almost identical: all showed a huge lightning strike through my arm. The doctor told me that scar tissue had grown between the split in the bone, meaning I'd lost some of my flexibility, about 10 to 12 degrees worth.

I was then given a few options. I could have had the arm broken again and reset. I was assured it was a safe operation, but I wasn't too keen to play around with it. I was back to bowling quickly, and although there was pain there it wasn't worrying me that much. I had a good chat to Dad, and he said having the arm reset might affect my bowling and it could be worse than if I just left it alone. So we decided, even though there was some pain there to leave the arm the way it was.

It frustrates me that the fracture wasn't picked up in Hobart. Not being able to straighten my arm might have cost me some pace. And it certainly caused me some worries a few years later when I was reported for throwing in the 2000 Tests against New Zealand.

Even now there are days when the arm is really sore, especially in cold weather. There are a whole lot of weights exercises I can't do, like triceps curls. I've hardly touched a weight since the injury. There has always been a lump there, and always some pain.

Despite the ongoing worries about his arm during the 1993–94 season, Brett continued his march towards higher honours. In his debut first-grade season for Campbelltown he took 14 wickets at 26.86, a promising enough return for officials to suggest their teenage paceman was:

A very big prospect for Australian cricket. Joined first grade for the first of the one-day games, and then straight into the 2 day team for round four. Has genuine pace which will worry all batsmen in years to come. (*Campbelltown Year Book*, 1993–94)

Brett's best figures for the grade season were 4–56 against northern Sydney club Gordon, which included NSW wicket-keeper Phil Emery. Emery remembers:

Brett was the fastest bowler I'd seen in grade since Geoff Lawson. His control was amazing; he knew what he was doing all the time. And he was only 16! His first two balls to me were short and wide outside off-stump, which I cut for four. He picked up the challenge and said, 'Is that the only shot you've got?' It was pretty game for a 16-year-old to say anything. We had a few words, then I thought to myself, 'I'm not going to say any more because this kid is only going to get faster and I'm only going to get slower.' He was something special, and from that day on I expected to hear and see a lot more about him.

NSW batsman Richard Chee Quee was also stunned by Brett's pace when Campbelltown was at home to Randwick at Raby Oval. Brett finished wicket-less, but left his marks on Chee Quee and a top order that also included State players Rod Davison and Martin Haywood. Chee Quee recalls:

He was very, very, very quick, but he didn't have the strength or the stamina that he has got now, which meant he tired more quickly. But we still had to handle his first five overs. And those overs were as fast as I had ever seen or faced. It was in about the third over of the day when Brett bowled this ball to me on a good length that I decided to go forward to, as you normally do. But the ball just rose from nowhere and I had to fend it off my grill, it just clipped my glove on the way through. I heard this big appeal, and normally I'd start to walk. But I looked around and the umpire had his arm out after calling no-ball. It was the only time in my career that I actually thought 'oh no'. I would have been quite happy to have gone off. By this stage Brett was running through to the keeper to celebrate before he'd heard the umpire's call. When he saw what had happened, he looked pretty angry. As he walked back past me he said something like: 'I'll get you next time.' I just quietly told him, 'You're just not good enough. Get back to your mark and stop f. . . ing cheating!' I was referring to the no-ball. Later on he hit Davo [Rod Davison] a few times in the ribs and also broke Martin Haywood's finger. We ended up getting the better of him that day, but we couldn't forget him. He was faster than fast.

The highlight of the season came when Brett was named in the Australian Under-19 team for a tour of India in February and March '94. The selection caused a predicament for the Lee family because Brett had begun Year 12 and was studying for his Higher School Certificate. However, after talking with his parents and principal, Brett took his books on the tour with him. This was his introduction to international cricket and, as team-mate Corey Richards recalls, it was also an indication of what Test batsmen would face within a few years:

I first played with Brett when we were at Campbelltown together. At first he was known as Shane Lee's brother, but it took no time to realise he was something exceptional. He was quick and rushing established players. The game against Randwick was unforgettable. I've never seen anything like it. I was at second slip, and Brett was absolutely rapid. I hadn't seen his sheer pace until that time. And all of a sudden Shane's younger brother had a reputation all to himself as possibly the fastest bowler in Australia, but half the Australian players wouldn't have even heard of him.

On the Indian tour he was really intimidating despite the slow decks. He was as aggressive as anyone I'd ever seen. In one game when I was captain, there was this one batsman we couldn't get out. We were all getting really frustrated; Brett was really firey, and had 'steam coming out of his ears'. I was standing at mid-off when Brett eventually came across and said, 'I'm going to run through the crease and hurt this guy.' I didn't believe he was going to do it, but he was just seeing red. So next ball, he ran through and hit this poor little guy under the ribs. The batsman, who was no more than 5 feet tall, went down like a sack of spuds and he had to be taken off, and we ended up winning the game.

In a team which included Jason Gillespie, Matt Nicholson, Mike Hussey and Andrew Symonds, Brett was one of the best performers. His most commanding effort came in the Third, and final, Test against the Indian Under-19s in Bombay. He took 4–61 and 4–70 in the Australians' six-wicket win. The series was drawn 1–1.

After returning home, he followed the same path as his older brother by earning a tier-two scholarship to the Australian Cricket Academy. It meant he spent a busy winter combining trips to Adelaide with his HSC studies, although it was obvious where his interests lay. On the cricket field he'd already proven he was dedicated and determined, however, he admits his mind was often elsewhere in the classroom, where he was renowned for being a fidgeter who couldn't sit still for any length of time.

After finishing school in October '94, he was able to concentrate full-time on cricket during the '94–95 season. His first grade season set the standard: 27 wickets at 28.2 from 13 matches. Campbelltown was nurturing a star:

Started to show real signs of becoming the fastest bowler in NSW or perhaps even Australia, and on occasions was a terrifying sight to opposition batsmen. He has the right temperament and is developing a genuine dislike for batsmen, a trait shared by Lillee and Thomson. (Campbelltown Year Book, 1994–95)

Representative selections came as quickly as his bowling: He was chosen in both the NSW Colts and Under-19 teams, and was once again a member of the national Under-19s, which hosted a return series against India.

New Zealand's future Test hopefuls also experienced Lee's speed when the Australian Cricket Academy played their trans-Tasman rivals at Hamilton. The game was given first-class status, opening the door for many of the players, including Brett, to make their debuts at that level. Brett took 1–48 and 3–71 in the Australians' 10-wicket victory.

It was inevitable that Brett would be part of the Academy's full-time intake for the '95 winter. Among the 14 players chosen was Jason Gillespie, the wiry 20-year-old South Australian who within five years would form, with Brett and Glenn McGrath, one of cricket's most threatening Test pace-attacks. Both Brett and Jason, however, were to suffer from serious injuries. For Brett, the sign of things to come first happened when the Academy toured Pakistan in September 1995:

The tour was pretty hectic. It was very hot and I bowled quite a few overs. During one of the games, I felt this terrible pain in the back while I was bowling. I bowled another ball, stopped, bowled again, and stopped again. It was getting worse and worse, and my back started to seize up. It felt like a knife was driving into my lower spine and twisting. It was excruciating.

I came home to see specialists in Wollongong and Adelaide, and they all came up with the same conclusion: that I had hot spots, which are areas where there are stress fractures or about to be stress fractures. Scans revealed I had problems in both the L2 and L3 parts of the back. These are quite high for fast bowlers because most get injuries around L4 and L5.

The injuries made me think of when I'd bowled in front of Dennis Lillee for the first time at a young paceman's clinic in Sydney. I was just 15 and trying to impress him by bowling as quickly as I could. But he pulled me aside and said although I had good pace, I had a mixed action which meant my bottom half was side on, and my top half was front on. He told me that led to counter rotation of the hips, and placed added stress on the lower back. Then he gave me the warning that I'll never forget: 'I hope it doesn't happen, but if you don't work on your action, it's possible that you will break down in the next three or four years.' I was shattered, but being so young I didn't listen. I'd been taking wickets, and loved bowling as fast as I could. What could go wrong? So I kept playing, but then the prediction came true. Bang! I was gone.

Lillee, too, remembers the early meeting, and the unfortunate prediction:

Brett was very, very quick. He broke a stump at one stage, and you have to be fast to do that. He was also eager to soak up any information he could, and he had this look on his face that told me he was willing to try things.

You don't always see those traits in coaching. You hope for them, but you don't always get them. He certainly made me sit up and take notice, but I was concerned about his action. I suggested there and then it would be a good idea to try to remodel his action and make it safer. But I can understand a young bloke at 15 years of age not wanting to listen to an old bloke predicting gloom and doom. We all have that invincible feeling at that age.

I don't take any pleasure in seeing predictions like that come true, but I could see that with his mixed action, the pace he bowled at, the pressure he put on his back, and the call he'd have to bowl more and more overs, a breakdown was inevitable.

Brett was forced to rest. In the hope of enhancing his recovery he undertook a Pilates course, a method of training that helps improve the body's lower core strength and flexibility, and after four months of sitting beyond the boundary he was allowed to resume playing, but only as a batsman — he didn't bowl throughout the 1995–96 season. His duties were restricted to just five middle-order innings with a top score of 51 not out in second grade for his new club, Mosman.

The 1995–96 season proved to be a very mixed one for the Lees: Brett played little cricket; Grant was selected in the NSW Under-17 team and continued the family tradition; and Shane discovered the answer to his prayers in Adelaide.

CHAPTER SIX

THE ALL-ROUND AUSSIE

Lee is the way of the future.
Phil Wilkins, *Sydney Morning Herald*, 13 December 1995

Potential. What does it mean? Is a sportsman blessed if he has it? Or is it a curse that can weigh heavily on the mind until the ability is realised? If it ever is.

When Victorian all-rounder Simon O'Donnell departed the international scene in 1991–92, the search had already begun for a replacement. Someone who could hit the ball hard and often, take wickets but still be frugal, and field like a drover's dog rounding up a mob of sheep. Someone who could be a matchwinner. Someone with *potential*. It was a word that often shared the same sentence with Shane, even from his earliest cricketing days, and when he entered the first-class arena there was a lot of speculation in the media about whether the 'new O'Donnell' had been discovered.

The 1995–96 season loomed as a critical one in Shane's career. After being relegated to twelfth man for the final match of the previous Shield season, he had to recover lost ground. The first step came during the off-season when he was approached by Mosman officials to join their northern Sydney club. It was a package deal that included his brother Brett, and after discussing it with him Shane decided the change of club was a good idea for both of their cricketing futures. Mosman was closer to the SCG, and would cut down the travel time to training and matches. It was a relief to Shane who, after spending his formative years clocking thousands of kilometres, was now a local to the area, having moved the previous year. Higher-level commitments, however, restricted his first grade season to just four matches, during which his best return with the ball was 5–47 and his top score was 47.

Under NSW coach Geoff Lawson, Shane was selected for the Blues' first outing of the season: a game at Sydney's Hurstville Oval against touring South African team Western Province. It proved a memorable start. He slammed 84 off 90 balls in the first innings and remained unbeaten on 67 in the second, after sharing a 178-run stand in just 122 minutes with Michael Bevan (122 not out). Aided by his remarkable batting and bowling — Shane also took 2–5 in the first innings — NSW won by 126 runs. Such a return gave the young NSW all-rounder a much-needed shot of confidence:

Self-belief is a really individual thing. It doesn't only apply to cricket, but to everything we do, whether it be work, relationships or sport.

Some people are really confident from the start, probably too confident. To others like me, confidence doesn't come naturally. It only comes from success, and focusing on the right things; you can't focus on anything negative, and the most important part is to enjoy whatever you're doing. In my first few years I put too much pressure on myself, and in hindsight I probably made every match out to be a much bigger occasion than it actually was.

The 1995–96 season was my fourth in first-class cricket, and although I was determined to come back strongly after the disappointing finish to the previous year, I was really conscious of trying to relax and have a bit more fun.

Steve Waugh was a great help. I took strength from his experience at the start of his career when it wasn't easy for him. Back then big things were expected of him, but he also copped a fair bit of bagging. Because of that, he understands better than any other player what young guys have to go through to make the grade. Some reach the top and click straight away, but I wasn't like that, and when talking with Steve I could relate to what he went through. That in itself gave me some confidence.

However, Shane's opening matches of the domestic season brought no notable returns. He scored 19 and failed to take a wicket in the Blues' 11-run Mercantile Mutual Cup victory against Queensland at North Sydney Oval. He again went wicket-less and scored 6, and 10 not out, when NSW drew its first Shield outing of the summer with Western Australia in Perth. But the day after that match, he claimed 4–59 as the Blues strolled to a seven-wicket win over the Warriors in the Mercantile Mutual Cup. It was the beginning of a golden patch that was highlighted by a brilliant all-round performance against Tasmania at the SCG. In a full-strength NSW team which beat the Tigers by 214 runs, Shane upstaged the Waugh brothers and Michael Slater by scoring an unbeaten 101 in the first innings, and sharing an unbroken 184-run stand with Michael Bevan (103 not out). Just as they had done three weeks earlier against Western Province, Shane and Bevan set a blistering pace, 151 runs coming in the final session on the opening day. Shane recalls:

Bevo and I were developing a really good understanding. He reads games so well, and always gives good advice. You get extra value for your shots when batting with him because he is such a good runner between the wickets. He always puts a lot of pressure on the fieldsmen: quick singles suddenly seem easy, and easy twos suddenly become possible threes. When that happens, bowlers can get really frustrated, especially when there is a right- and left-hand combination. Bevo made it even harder for them because he is such a freakish batsman. When he has to score quick runs, he has two or three shots for every ball.

Going into that season, we both had different but in many ways similar aims. Bevo wanted to impress the Australian selectors after a bit of time out of the team, and I wanted to show the NSW selectors that I had a lot more to give, and I was determined I was never going to be dropped to twelfth man again. At that stage I wasn't thinking beyond State cricket. I know there were a lot of people expecting me to take another step up, but it really was the old saying of taking one game at a time.

After my century I was really keen to have a bowl, but only ended up having six overs in the first innings. Glenn McGrath and Simon Cook took three wickets each in the opening attack, and I wasn't called on until after Greg Matthews, David Freedman and Bevo had spells.

But my chance came in the second innings after Michael Slater had scored 100 not out, and we'd set Tasmania 384 to win. The final day was really hot, and by the time I came on at the fortieth over, the ball was starting to reverse swing [swing Irish]. It was a typical time for the ball to start going Irish in Sydney. And it really helped me. I took 4–20 off 11 overs. Greg Matthews helped start it when he took a great diving catch at short cover to get rid of Shaun Young. I then caught and bowled David Boon with a slower ball, two balls later Michael DiVenuto was lbw, and then I had Rod Tucker caught behind in the next over. It was the best I'd bowled, and as we were walking off I thought to myself, 'About bloody time!' I'd not only shown others, but also myself that I could bowl successfully at this level.

Shane had chosen a near-perfect stage on which to perform well because there were few more important people to impress in Australian cricket than captain Mark Taylor. Taylor had already shown his faith in his young all-rounder earlier in the season when he gave Shane the responsibility of bowling out the final overs in the Mercantile Mutual Cup match against Queensland. The World Cup on the subcontinent was just four months away, and a bowler with the ability to reverse swing the ball in the final overs of an innings would be a prized asset on the slow, dusty wickets of India, Sri Lanka and Pakistan. Shane says:

The first time I remember bowling reverse swing was at Oak Flats. I actually couldn't work out what was happening. No-one spoke about it; it was just happening. But when I moved into the NSW squad, Mike Whitney and Wayne Holdsworth taught me the theory behind it. It was crucial to be able to bowl it at the SCG where the ball normally got scuffed up pretty quickly. There were all these theories about loading one side of the ball with spit, so it became much heavier than the other side. But it was much more than that. You still had to really work on shining the ball.

At training, I used to practise by rubbing one side of a ball against the bricks until it was scuffed up like it would be in a match. I'd then shine up the other side and experiment in the nets. It took a few seasons to get the hang of it, and is probably now the easiest form of swing bowling because I don't really have to worry about wrist positions or the action. I just have to worry about what line I want to start with. It takes a lot of practice. It's easier to get the ball to swing in than go away. I've discovered I have to bowl with a much higher action, but every bowler is different. There's no set way or textbook when it comes to swinging Irish. Trying to bowl it can be very frustrating because sometimes the ball doesn't go at all. But there's no doubt bowlers are becoming better and better at using it. Like the Pakistanis. Look at Waqar Younis. He's awesome.

The fact that I was quite comfortable bowling Irish was a plus for World Cup selection, but I knew I still had to perform in every game if I was going to be a part of Australia's plans.

Shane maintained his bowling momentum for the next encounter: a six-wicket win over Victoria in a Shield contest at the MCG. He had a match return of 3–71 off 26.2 overs, and in his only innings he scored 20. After taking 1–28 off 8 overs in the ensuing Mercantile Mutual Cup win over the Victorians, he again tormented Tasmania with Shield innings of 63, and 33 not out, in the Blues' 109-run triumph at Bellerive Oval. He took only one wicket, but his earlier performances had already left a telling impression on the national selectors. His step-up came swiftly and surprisingly:

The game against Tasmania was my last before the Australian squad was chosen for the World Series against the West Indies and Sri Lanka. There had been some talk in the papers that I had a chance of being selected, but I didn't believe it. I was just happy that I was finally proving that I belonged in the NSW team, and was being given more responsibility. When I went on a promotional trip with some of the Blues to Coffs Harbour in mid-December, I didn't even know the national team was being chosen while I was away. And then all of a sudden I found myself in Adelaide training with the Aussies and preparing for my first international against the West Indies.

Having so many NSW players in the squad made me feel more comfortable. Bevo and I joined Tubby [Mark Taylor], Mark Waugh and Glenn McGrath. It was like being at an instant coaching clinic. I just learnt by watching everyone, and how they reacted to different situations.

Although everyone made me feel really welcome, it was still a tough time because I knew I was on show. Luckily, I did well in the first match, but struggled after that. Once again I suffered from putting too much pressure on myself and I was forgetting to enjoy the game. I'd done well to get rid of that mentality at State level, but this was a whole new ball game.

I got caught up in thinking I immediately had to outdo every other all-rounder who was trying to get into the squad. That added to the pressure. Looking back, if I'd had more experience I would have just concentrated on doing my own job. The moment you start worrying about what others are doing is the moment when your own game suffers.

It was strange the different things that disturbed me. There were times when I'd walk back to the top of my mark, and I'd realise there'd be a camera on my face, and that made me very conscious of what I was doing. It's amazing the things that went through my head: Were my mates at Mount Warrigal watching? What were Mum and Dad thinking? How many people were sitting in their lounge rooms at home thinking I didn't belong there? I should have been thinking about anything but those things, but it was easier said than done.

I was very relieved after my first game went well, but I knew the eyes were still on me when we played a day/nighter against the West Indies two

This boy has potential! Helen and Bob Lee with Brett before his first representative game for the South Coast.

Putting the best foot forward. Brett and Shane prepare for their first one-day international together during the 1999–2000 season.

Shane listens to self-confessed 'cricket tragic', John Howard after leading the Prime Minister's XI to victory over India (1999–2000).

'To make this work, one of us has to reverse swing!' A typical day at the Lee household.

'I bat, you bowl.' Shane lays down the backyard rules to Brett from an early age.

Hat-trick! The three brothers. Shane, Brett and Grant.

Which is mightier? The ball? Or the bat? By the time he was in late primary school, Brett had made his choice to be a fast bowler.

Shane in his first leadership role.

Shane playing the clown with Brett and Grant. Behind them, is the roller door that received a hammering from the driveway cricket matches.

ALLSPORT

NEWS LIMITED

'You make me want to shout!' Shane enjoys taking a wicket against the Western Warriors.

Seek and destroy! Brett in a position that has become a frightening sight for batsmen the world over.

ALLSPORT

Shane with the pose made famous by Dennis Lillee.

Shane opening the bowling in his Sheffield Shield debut against Western Australia at the SCG (1992–93).

Brett considers his options at the top of his mark.

'Got him!' Steve Waugh joins Shane in celebrations after Courtney Walsh is the final wicket to fall in Australia's 20 run victory over the West Indies at Port of Spain, Trinidad (1999).

Brett and his namesake, the very successful NSW Greyhound. Both speedsters have endured their share of injuries.

Brett poses with Paula Joye (*Cleo* Editor) for the cameras after being named runner-up in the 2000 *Cleo* Bachelor of the Year. The winner, David Whitehill, is pictured right.

Shane is alone with his thoughts while bowling for Australia 'A'.

The speed machine. Brett in full stride during his international debut summer (1999–2000).

Stress point. The body is put under most pressure at the point of delivery. Brett knows better than many cricketers just how damaging this can be.

Cricket is a great leveller. Shane's prodigious talents are brought back to the field in a game of 'Blind Cricket' in Worcester before Australia's World Cup campaign began in England (1999).

Brett on the end of a thunderbolt during the Australia v West Indies Test Series 2000–2001.

days later in Melbourne. We batted first, and I came in at number 7 when we were trying to pick up the pace in the final overs. I felt confident after Adelaide, and when I walked onto the ground I got a big cheer, which gave me a little more confidence. I'd been hitting the ball really well in the nets and was determined to make an impact, but after making 3, I picked up a ball from Curtly Ambrose off my pads and was caught by Shivnarine Chanderpaul at deep backward square-leg. I bowled first change and took 1–40 off 10 overs. We ended up winning by 24 runs, and although my contribution was small, I still felt OK.

I had limited chances in the next day/nighter against Sri Lanka in Sydney. I repeated my Melbourne bowling figures, 1–40 again. My scalp was an important one — Aravinda De Silva caught and bowled for 75. We were chasing 256 to win, and we got the runs with only two balls to spare when Bevo hit a boundary off Kumara Dharmasena. I was at the other end on 4 not out. It was great to be in the centre when we won, especially since it was in front of my home crowd. I was also happy for Bevo; he hadn't done anything wrong since coming back into the team. Being dropped can be a real motivator, and it certainly was for Bevo.

And relegation was soon to test Shane's character. In his next three matches he took one wicket and tallied six runs from two innings. It was no surprise that Shane was the casualty when Steve Waugh returned from a hamstring injury. He was dropped to twelfth man for the day/nighter against Sri Lanka in Perth, which was to be the closest he came to playing another international for the rest of the home season. However, selectors kept faith in his ability by retaining him in the squad that defeated Sri Lanka 2–0 in a finals series that will sadly be remembered for its bitterness. The second final in Sydney included a series of ugly incidents: Glenn McGrath and opener Sanath Jarasuriya engaged in a mid-pitch push and shove match; Ian Healy had a short but heated exchange with Arjuna Ranatunga when the Sri Lankan captain called for a runner despite appearing uninjured; and, after the match, the Sri Lankans refused to shake hands with many of the Australians or acknowledge the home team when it was presented with the trophy. The explosive incidents proved an omen for what would soon follow.

In the meantime, Australia announced its 14-member squad for the World Cup which was to begin in three weeks. Despite his slide in form during the World Series, Shane was among the players chosen by Trevor Hohns and his committee.

In his only hit out before Australia left for the subcontinent, he took one wicket and scored 69, and 22 not out, in a drawn day/night Shield match against Western Australia in Sydney.

The day after the match finished, the uneasy relationship between Australia and Sri Lanka suffered greater strains after a suicide bomb attack by Tamil terrorists killed more than 100 people in Colombo. The site was just a few minutes' walk from where Taylor's men were due to stay in little more than a week's time as they prepared for their opening Cup match against the host nation. When combined with the revelations that Shane Warne, Craig McDermott and coach Bob Simpson had recently received death threats, the Australians were understandably concerned about touring Sri Lanka. They'd already voiced their worries in meetings with Australian Cricket Board officials before the bombing, and the latest episode gave the ACB only one, controversial, option: abort the Sri Lankan leg of the campaign, and forfeit the points. The West Indies, who were also due to play in Sri Lanka, followed Australia's lead. The decisions were condemned by Sri Lankan officials and PILCOM, the tournament's official organising committee.

Shane recalls:

It was a tough time for everyone. We were talking a lot amongst ourselves, and although some of the guys didn't want to go, others who'd been there before were saying we'd be all right. Being my first tour for Australia, I probably still would have gone if the bomb had gone off in our hotel! I was just so keen to play a part.

But there's no doubt the ACB made the right decision because nothing should ever stand in the way of human safety. Before we left we were assured we were going to have the best security with extra guards employed by the ACB in addition to the protection offered by Cup organisers. Although that made us feel more comfortable, no-one could really assure us that our safety could be 100 per cent guaranteed.

But once we were over there, we learnt to accept it. Everywhere we went there were guards with guns surrounding us. Our hotel floors were under 24-hour security, and at some hotels guests and visitors had to walk through metal detectors before being allowed in. At first it was pretty off-putting. Terrorism is unfortunately part of life on the subcontinent, but it was all a new experience for us.

Having all the security did have some funny sides. Quite often we'd go past a bodyguard with a gun, then all of a sudden he'd pull out an autograph book and forget all about the job he was meant to be doing.

The tour was a tremendous learning curve for me. When I first got to Sydney airport with the team I was really excited. It was like starting a new chapter in my career. Coming in as a young guy on my first tour, I was really aware of not interrupting anyone else's routine. I just wanted to do the simple things well. Like make sure I was always on time for everything the team did, whether it be training, official functions or bus trips. I was also conscious of wearing the right gear, which wasn't a hard thing to do because I was so proud of what I was doing.

Obviously there were guys like Steve Waugh and Mark Taylor who'd been touring for years and knew exactly what was expected. But for me, nearly everything was new. I couldn't stop thinking about the games ahead; I knew I had to perform well. There were still a lot of people watching, waiting to see how I went at this level.

To help relax and create a bit of fun for the team during free time, Bevo and I took our guitars over. Bevo was trying to learn the bass, and of course with a bass you also need an amplifier, so we were like a mini-band on tour. It wasn't always smooth going though. The first time we pulled out our guitars for a bit of a jam, I somehow broke one of Bevo's strings while trying to tune it. You could run the Blue Mountains cable car on a bass string, so I don't know how I snapped it. Bevo blew up as only he could; he completely lost it! Where was he going to get a replacement string? Luckily we found a string from a local band that was downstairs in the hotel. Then it was on. From that moment, the Bevan–Lee music show was a happening thing. We did little gigs and sing-a-longs that Michael Slater also got involved in. Slats fancies himself as a bit of a singer, so it was pretty funny to see these three Aussie guys in India trying to be as cool as INXS. We played in our rooms and on a couple of the longer bus trips, especially the six-hour ride to the Taj Mahal. It was just a fun thing to do. It was great. It made the time go quicker and created a good feeling among the team. I think the players quite enjoyed it. They didn't bag us too much!

The music also gave us a distraction from the touring life. It takes some time to acclimatise in India and adjust to the culture. There can be so many shocks that just hit you right in the face. There are people everywhere. And they nearly all love cricket. At every hotel we stayed at, it didn't take long for a cleaner or someone else from the hotel staff to come knocking on the door for autographs.

We stopped at Calcutta for the opening ceremony, and it took me a while to come to terms with how many beggars there were in the streets. It was just such a different way of life. As much as anything else on that trip, the street scenes taught me how much to appreciate Australia.

Because we forfeited the first World Cup game, we had nearly two weeks in India before we were into action. We made Bombay our base before moving on to Visakhapatnam for our match against Kenya. After my poor finish to the one-dayers at home I was desperate to get a start, but had to settle on carrying the drinks. I was disappointed because I wanted to get out on the field and make up for the poor returns of my final few matches.

We beat Kenya, and travelled to Bombay for our next game against India. Paul Reiffel had some bad luck when he was ruled out with a hamstring strain, but that meant good luck for me. It was great to finally get a chance, but the match wasn't an enjoyable one for me. I got hammered! 0–23 off 3 overs. Sachin Tendulkar smashed Glenn McGrath everywhere, then when Tubby came over to me and told me to start warming up, I immediately thought, 'Shit here we go!' He was no fun to bowl to at all. He improvised shots that few other people could play, and every time he hit a four the crowd would go mad. It was deafening, but an incredible experience. Tendulkar is definitely the best batsman I've ever bowled to.

Mark Waugh eventually had him stumped for 90. We were all really relieved, and that wicket helped set up our win by 16 runs.

We beat Zimbabwe by eight wickets in our next game, but I had little to do. I didn't have to bat, and took 0–8 off 4 overs. That was my last chance in the tournament because Pistol [Paul Reiffel] came back and kept his spot.

It was frustrating playing only two games, but it was difficult to dislodge a player like Pistol when he was fit. He was such a solid team player who rarely ever put a foot wrong in a match. Always dependable and consistent. Despite being a spectator, I still had a really good time. It was a very hard but enjoyable tour. My best memory is our semi-final win over the West Indies at Chandigarh. We were in all sorts of trouble at 4–15, but thanks to half-centuries by Stuart Law and Bevo we scraped together 207. That wasn't many, especially when the Windies cruised to 2–165, but then they fell in a heap and lost their last eight wickets for 37. When Damien Fleming bowled Courtney Walsh for the last wicket, I was so excited I sprinted onto the field from the dressing rooms, and Flem reckons I was the fourth person into the team huddle. I'd beaten nearly everyone on the field to join in the celebrations. It was a great feeling to be part of it, even though I wasn't playing.

Before that match we'd spoken in the team meeting about the West Indies being unable to 'take the gas', and that's exactly what happened.

After their escape in Chandigarh, the Australians were confident heading into the final against Sri Lanka in Lahore. However, Arjuna Ranatunga's men were seeking revenge for their last controversial meeting against Australia and swept to a seven-wicket victory on the back of an unbeaten century by Aravinda De Silva.

Shane returned home to take four wickets in the Blues' last Shield match of the season against eventual champions South Australia in

Sydney. The drawn match completed another lowly season for the second-last-placed NSW. However, by then Shane's thoughts were elsewhere. A surprise phone call before he left for the World Cup ensured the winter of 1996 was anything but an off-season:

Just before the World Cup I'd received a call from Bob Cottam, who was the director of cricket at Somerset. He asked me if I was interested in playing the '96 county season. I didn't believe it, but next thing you know he was in Australia watching me play a grade game at Waverley Oval. He signed me that afternoon. One of the first people I rang was Steve Waugh, who'd played for Somerset a few years earlier. I told him about the deal I'd been offered which was a £20 000 retainer plus incentives that were based on runs, wickets, and Somerset's position on the table. Steve said, 'Don't worry about the money. Just go over there and get the experience. It's a great opportunity for you.'

I was very excited because it was my first trip to England. And it came at a very important time in my career. I felt as though I had to start all over again because no-one had really seen me play or knew much about me. I also had the added responsibility of being the overseas player, which was a big ask considering I was replacing leg-spinner Mushtaq Ahmed, who was on tour in England with the Pakistan team. The previous season he'd bowled over 1000 overs and taken more than 100 wickets. I joked to the Somerset officials that if they expected me to bowl 1000 overs, I'd take up leg-spin too. But I don't think they were expecting that much from me. I was one of the lower-paid professionals, and I knew they were taking a bit of a punt on me.

At first I really didn't know whether I was ready for the challenge. As the overseas player I knew I had to perform straight away if I didn't want to cop a bagging. The opening game was on our home ground at Taunton against Surrey, who had Brendon Julian as their overseas professional. Despite BJ being an opponent, I felt at home knowing he was there. The match was a draw, but I was pleased with my own start. I made 87 in my only dig and took three wickets. It was a good way to kick off, and helped relieve a bit of pressure.

We played our first three championship games at home, which was good for my batting because Taunton is one of the flattest wickets I've ever played on. All you needed to do was hit the ball into the gap and it was four.

The third game against Northamptonshire was one of the highlights of my career because I scored 113 not out against an attack that included Curtly Ambrose. It was a real experience for me because Ambrose kept coming in and giving nothing away. He was at the batsmen all the time. I really worked hard on planning my innings, in a way I had not often done before. I started batting in tens and each time I got to a new mark I told myself to start all over again. I was beginning to think a lot more.

And that showed in other innings I played during the season. My top score, 167 not out, came against Worcestershire at Bath. I enjoyed that innings because it was against Tom Moody, who was one of my rivals for a spot in the Australian team. I didn't really know Tom at that stage, but there was a rivalry there. I bowled him for 20 in the first innings, but my bowling as a whole wasn't proving to be as successful or consistent as my batting. I'll remember that match the most because Worcestershire carved us up in the second innings to make 446, and win the match with one wicket in hand and three balls to spare.

Every match was teaching me something new, and as the season went on I was a lot more assured and confident. One of the most valuable lessons was against Derbyshire at Taunton. Dean Jones captained a pretty good bowling attack that included Devon Malcolm, Phil DeFreitas and Dominic Cork. It was a really flat wicket, and from the very start of my innings I felt in control, but I threw it all away. I made 110, and normally that's a score to take some satisfaction from, but I was really angry. I'd holed out, cutting a ball to third man off Malcolm. I walked off thinking I'd blown it. I should have scored 250! When I got back to the dressing room I sat down and made sure I'd remember the way I was feeling so that it would motivate me for future innings. Every batsman goes through enough low times to realise you have to make the most of the big scores when you get the chance. I look at a batsman like Steve Waugh, and his approach is the same no matter what his score. He is there to bat, and it's up to the bowlers to get him out because he'll rarely give his wicket away.

Not only was I learning new things about my game, but I was also learning a lot about myself. About three-quarters of the way through the season my form started to drop off a bit. The reason was simple: I was beginning to drop off. It was hard to get motivated for every game. There's no doubt they play too much cricket in England. With all the one-day competitions on top of the county commitments, players are out in the middle virtually every day; and when they're not playing, they're driving to the next game. There are a lot of good players over there, but it's physically and mentally impossible to be up for every match if you're playing five to six days a week. It's easy to lose hunger and intensity, and it started happening to me. I got to the stage where I didn't want to get out of bed. I'd wake up thinking, 'Oh shit, I don't want to go out and field all day again.' I really started looking forward to the batting days when I could sit around and look after the niggling injuries that were creeping in because of the sheer weight of cricket I was playing. I wasn't interested in bowling, and I started to get a few low scores. It was a tough time. I knew I really had to pull myself together because as the overseas player I was always expected to be at the top of my game. I had a long think and realised I could finish the season in one of two ways: I could let the grind get the better of me, and finish on a downer and have an average season; or I could pick myself up and get on top of everything. Luckily I did that. And one of my last matches turned out to be one of my best when I scored 126 and took 4–52 bowling first change against Sussex.

Looking back, it's really hard to compare English cricket with Australian cricket because they are two very different structures, but there's no doubt the English system I played under was much softer than the one I was used to back home. One of the most noticeable problems on the county circuit was that players were re-signed as early as three-quarters of the way through the season and, once the guys knew they were safe, some started to relax a bit.

The really good players stood out. The hardest batsman I bowled to was Graham Gooch, who scored 200 against us for Essex. He was so disciplined. He only had a few shots but he left me with little room for error; anything near his pads was through the gaps, and it was all over for me if I bowled anything too short or full.

It's not surprising the two stand-out bowlers were Courtney Walsh and Curtly Ambrose. They were in a different league to every other bowler I faced. Waqar Younis was also exceptional, although I didn't face him for long because he broke one of my fingers with a short ball before I'd scored in the match against Pakistan. I retired for 0 and made a duck in the second innings, but I was pleased to get 4–65. It is always rewarding to perform well against international teams, no matter what the occasion.

There's no doubt that the whole county experience was an important moulding point in my career. It was good preparation for Australia because the weight of games and travelling helped discipline me: when you're playing and travelling nearly all the time, you really have to know when to switch on and off. I also had the chance to experiment more than I had in Sheffield Shield and Mercantile Mutual Cup games. That was one of the biggest advantages of the whole trip, especially in the one-dayers. I told Somerset I was used to bowling the final overs for NSW — I'd actually only done it a couple of times — but I wanted to put my hand up for it. I ended up playing that role in most matches, which taught me more about variation with slower balls and yorkers. I was beginning to think a lot more, and was ready to return to Australia with a few new weapons. Despite playing non-stop for nearly a year, I felt fresh and very confident.

His confidence was supported by the statistics. Shane finished on top of Somerset's championship batting aggregates and averages with 1300 runs at 65, including five centuries and an equal number of fifties. Although unable to match Mushtaq Ahmed's phenomenal returns with the ball, he still had the respectable yield of 36 wickets, albeit at the expensive average of 47.36. But his efforts weren't enough to lift his team into contention, Somerset finished eleventh with five wins, six losses, and six draws, nor did the county figure strongly in the seemingly endless list of limited-overs tournaments. Shane's most memorable performance in the shortened matches came in the 60-overs-a-side Natwest Trophy competition when he was awarded Man of the Match against Suffolk after racing to 104 off 103 balls.

His batting throughout the season prompted high praise from *Wisden's Almanack* (1997), the cricketers' 'bible':

The greatest playing bonus came from Lee. Members will remember his season fondly; his classical driving and general competence often revived the batting, always lifted the scoring rate and several times completely turned a match.

Shane was just 23 when he returned home after his English stint. After the most rewarding 12 months of his career, it seemed Australian cricket had found an all-rounder who was indeed 'the way of the future'.

CHAPTER SEVEN

FIELD OF DREAMS

*People now play for the Oak Flats Cricket Club because of
Shane and Brett. Young kids want to try to follow them.
We're all very proud of them, but we never let
them know it!*

Kerry Penfold, family friend

Two teams of spindle-legged boys form one pack as they hunt a
soccer ball that bounces from one shin to the next, only
occasionally making solid contact with a well-timed boot. The boys'
oversized red and blue shirts hang from their bodies like kites
waiting for a good breath of wind, and their baggy shorts and long
socks are so big that they almost join, allowing only thin strips of
skin to be seen just below the knees. On the sidelines, more
comfortably attired parents stand, sit, shout and are silent. Behind
them, a simple wooden sign bolted to two posts stretches
horizontally above the ground at a height similar to the soccer
players, who continue chasing the ball with the same vigour seen in
the Lee boys when they played here. In those days it was known as
Panorama Oval, but since the sign was unveiled in late 1996 the
Oak Flats ground has been the Shane Lee Field. While Shane's

fame, locally, seemed set to endure, it did not look so certain in the minds of national selectors. After his international debut, and his experience at Somerset, Shane had every reason to be confident heading into the 1996–97 home season. But just as it appeared he was ready to be a regular member of Australia's limited-overs squad, and a Test hopeful, he was overlooked for the entire season. First, he missed selection for a one-day tournament in Sri Lanka in August, when Western Australia's left-hand batsman and wrist-spinner, Brad Hogg, was the surprise inclusion. Then, Hogg also toured India in October for the one-off Test that Australia lost heavily.

While the Australians were facing up to the challenges of the subcontinent, Shane opened his season by taking 5–32 against Parramatta at Mosman's Allan Border Oval. Although low key, it was an important start because he acknowledged his bowling had to improve if he was to force his way back into Australian colours:

I'd started my career as an opening bowler, but I knew if I was to do the business that season it would be as a change bowler. Having had a good season at Somerset, I was really keen to set the world on fire at home, but it didn't work out that way. Although I had my good moments, I just wasn't consistent. It was really frustrating. I kept telling myself that I was young and would get another opportunity somewhere along the line, but once again I started putting too much pressure on myself. For the previous 18 months I'd worked so hard on trying to relax and to just enjoy what I was doing, but then all of a sudden I was stressing myself out.

There were times when I thought back to my last one-day game for Australia when Sachin Tendulkar smashed me. I kept thinking that those 3 overs for 23 runs were the reason I was out of the team. I wanted to prove that I was much better than my last performance, but it was hard when I wasn't getting a chance.

It was a strange season for Shane. He started off reasonably well with the bat, opening his Shield account with two forties in the Blues' 58-run win over Victoria at the Sydney Cricket Ground.

However, success with the ball was much harder to come by. He took a wicket in each of his first three Mercantile Mutual Cup games, but didn't claim a Shield scalp until after Christmas. There was no better example of his fluctuating fortunes than when he scored an unbeaten 101 in the drawn match against Tasmania at Bellerive Oval, but was dropped for the next NSW Shield game because selectors couldn't squeeze him in among the returning Test contingent of Mark Taylor, the Waugh brothers, and Glenn McGrath. In the meantime, Tom Moody had been chosen as the all-rounder in Australia's one-day squad for the newly named Carlton United Series against Pakistan and the West Indies.

Although on the outer, Shane reminded everyone of his talents when he followed his Shield century with a chanceless 113 from just 103 balls in a one-day match against England 'A' at the SCG. It was his first limited-overs century for New South Wales, but the most telling statistic was that he took 0–47 off 10 overs in a match where the English sneaked to victory by two wickets with three balls remaining. Shane says:

That century against England was my best innings of the season. There is just something about playing an English team that makes every Australian player lift. But my bowling was still disappointing. Admittedly I wasn't getting many long spells because our spinners — Greg Matthews, Gavin Robertson, and David Freedman — were doing a lot of work. But when I did get the chance, I struggled to get into a groove.

Getting dropped from the NSW team after my two centuries was the most annoying part of the whole year. I could accept that I'd been overlooked for the Australian team, but it was really hard to think that I wasn't good enough to hold down my State spot, even with the Test players available. And again it was because my bowling wasn't up to scratch. Mark Taylor took me aside and told me I deserved to be in the team but that they needed another bowler, and Brad McNamara was chosen ahead of me because he'd been performing better. Tubby handled it very well; he understood how disappointed I was, but he was full of encouragement.

That's what made him such a respected captain — he was a really good communicator.

The selectors' support of McNamara was justified. A close friend of Lee's, McNamara eventually finished the season as the Blue's leading wicket-taker in both the Sheffield Shield and Mercantile Mutual Cup competitions. It wasn't until his sixth Shield match of the season, in late January, that Shane had reason to smile about his bowling. Gaining considerable reverse swing in humid conditions at the SCG, he took 3–15 and 3–32 as NSW crushed South Australia by an innings and 169 runs. The haul yielded half of Shane's Shield wickets for the season. His batting, although more rewarding, did not produce the same results as the season in Somerset: In nine Shield matches, he scored 506 runs at 33.73. NSW finished third after securing four outright victories. In the Mercantile Mutual Cup, the Blues lost to Queensland by 17 runs in a semi-final in Brisbane. Shane took 2–56 and fell for 3, caught behind off Michael Kasprowicz. It was a disappointing finish to a six-match campaign that returned 129 runs and 8 wickets.

However, a much more profitable season once again beckoned overseas. Although Somerset had re-signed Mushtaq Ahmed, leaving Shane without a county deal, he was keen to play in England during an Ashes year as he readily accepted an offer to be the professional at Enfield, a Lancashire League club that had previously hosted four Australians, including Damien Fleming. Shane replaced West Indian Franklyn Rose. Shane recalls:

I had a very eventful start to my stint. There always seems to be rumours going around small English towns, and when a pro comes in all the locals are keen to find out what the pro is like, what he does, what he gets up to socially. When Brad McNamara and I arrived — Buzzard was playing for Haslingden in the same league — there was already a rumour going around that Buzzard and I had been arrested on coming into England. But no-one knew what for. The rumour was so strong that it even got back to Australia. I remember Pat Farhart ringing from NSW Cricket to find out what had happened. He'd heard we'd been thrown in jail. I've got no idea how it started, but it was an entertaining way to make an impression upon the locals.

As far as the cricket went, the season was great fun, but I'd never do it again. It was ordinary cricket. I wouldn't recommend going over there with the aim of improving their game to any young player. It's a good experience, but it doesn't better your cricket.

Shane finished fourth in the League's batting averages with 802 runs at 44.56, and he took 67 wickets at 16.01. Enfield came third in the 14-team league. Despite his results, there was little importance placed on Shane's performances until a surprise phone call from Australian team manager Allan Crompton changed everything:

Allan told me I had to join up with the Australian team as soon as I could because Brendon Julian had been injured, and I'd been picked to play against Kent in a lead-up match to the final Test at the Oval. Shaun Young, who was playing county cricket, had also been included. We were to have a 'bowl off' in the match, and whoever was more impressive was expected to be picked in the Test side. It was hard to believe, and if it hadn't happened to Mike Whitney years before when he was promoted from the league ranks to a Test match in 1981, I would have thought someone was playing a trick on me.

But it was all true, so Shaun and I went head to head on a really flat wicket that I'd been smashed on the previous year when playing for Somerset. I was really nervous. It was the best opportunity I'd ever been presented with, and I kept telling myself that I was going to go and bowl so well that they'd have to pick me. I took four wickets in each innings, and bowled as well as I ever had. Shaun took two for the match. At the end I thought, 'I'm gonna fluke a Test match here. Can you believe it?' It was the perfect example of being in the right place at the right time. But the night before the team was announced, Tugga [Steve Waugh] quietly told me *that he didn't think I was going to be picked, and Shaun would get the nod because he'd been playing county cricket. Tugga would have known. It was his way of letting me know gently, which was a very considerate move. I wasn't upset, but I did feel disappointed. I thought I might have done enough to get included, but it wasn't to be.*

Off the field there was a much more significant issue developing at the time of the Kent match. Issues that had slowly begun developing as long ago as Australia's 1995 tour of the West Indies were slowly surfacing. During the Caribbean tour two years earlier, senior players had closely followed the split that developed in rugby league between the traditional competition that was run by the Australian Rugby League, and the breakaway Super League that was backed by Rupert Murdoch. The cricketers began comparing the differences in player payments and conditions between the codes. The results further enhanced a growing view that many of Australia's first-class players were underpaid, and consequently they needed a representative body to push their cause. Out of this, the Australian Cricketers' Association was re-formed in 1995.

Players' associations had come and gone since the 1970s, but the senior players were determined this latest one would become a powerful force. Tim May, who toured but didn't play a Test on the '95 Caribbean tour, accepted the role of union leader. For the next two years little progress was made, but then in 1997 the movement gained considerable momentum when the former Australian Cricket Board chief executive, Graham Halbish, was appointed to the Cricketers' Association payroll. Halbish had only been removed from his position at the beginning of the year, and his emergence as a key player for the cricketers created simmering unease between the ACA and the ACB. Halbish was soon joined by sports entrepreneur James Erskine, former head of Australian operations for the worldwide International Management Group (IMG) and the man who was to become the key negotiator for the ACA.

Erskine was introduced to the Australians while they were preparing for the Kent match. Shane recalls the clandestine nature of the meeting, and what would follow during the approaching Australian summer:

Everything was pretty well kept hush hush. All the big meetings started taking place at the time I was called up into the squad. Things really started happening the night before the Kent game when the team had a big talk with Erskine and Tim May. It was explained to us that a strategy had been mapped out, and James was going to negotiate for us. He said the bottom line was to get better payment for all of Australia's first-class players below the Test guys. Some players at that stage were on $5000 contracts, which was a pittance. There was a show of hands for support, and I couldn't help thinking, 'What is going on here?' I'd just been given the chance to play for Australia, and yet all my focus was being directed elsewhere. All I wanted to do was go out and play cricket, but there was no doubt this was a crucial meeting because we were basically voting on behalf of all Shield cricketers.

Tubby gave his view, but he was very careful about the words he chose. He said he believed a stronger voice for the cricketers was a good idea, but he didn't force his beliefs on anyone as captain. He said we all had to make up our own minds, but the fact the other senior players, Steve Waugh and Ian Healy, were also supportive had a big influence on some of the other players. A few guys asked questions about the whole process, and how much better off players would be if everything went according to plan. The aim was that the Cricketers' Association would consult with players' representatives before developing a list of proposals to take to the Australian Cricket Board.

There ended up being full support. And when we arrived back in Australia, we were kept updated by letters through the mail from Tim May.

As the 1997–98 Australian summer approached, Erskine, May and players' representatives finetuned a log of claims, which was presented to the ACB in October. An ugly battle had developed through the media, and May had refused to rule out strike action by players during the summer, an issue that was the talk of North Sydney Oval when NSW hosted Victoria the day after the claims had been presented. In recent times a Sheffield Shield match had rarely created so much interest: nearly every off-field movement by the players was monitored by a vast group of photographers and journalists who outnumbered the fans.

However, the most remarkable pictures from that game were taken on the field just before play began when both teams lined up shoulder to shoulder in an act of solidarity. It took many spectators by surprise, and even prompted a ground-staff member to stop rolling the pitch, believing the players were observing a minute's silence for someone.

Shane remembers:

It was a bizarre day. The line-up before play was a really big move. It was the first time we'd publicly stood up against officials. Greg Matthews, who was the NSW players' representative, was really pumped. When he told us that we were going to do the line-up, he said that it was for the union and that we had to stand by 'our brothers'. He said players had been 'shit on' for a long time, and things could only get better if we all stood together. He kept saying that no-one would come out of it worse off.

But no-one really knew the full story. We'd been finding out most of the developments through the papers and were left wondering, 'What the hell is going on with this?' We'd been fairly poorly informed, but in hindsight I understand why we weren't told much because when we were asked to do interviews with journalists there was nothing we could say. Basically we were just giving the line that we were all in this together, and we wanted our own strong voice.

There was growing talk about strikes, and I kept asking myself, 'If we do strike, will every player go with it?' That was my initial thought. I didn't doubt any of the players but, when it came down to it, cricket was where they earnt their money, and I wondered if everyone would stand together if the pressure was really on because some players would worry about the effects of taking on the officials.

But Greg Matthews reinforced all the way through that if there was one weak link the whole process would fall down, and we'd let our teammates down. Steve Waugh and Tubby were saying the same thing. One of the upcoming limited-overs internationals was apparently being targeted for strike action but, once again, no-one really knew for sure.

All we could do was play the game against Victoria and wait for further developments. As it turned out I had a pretty good game with the bat, scoring 81 not out in my only innings.

Shane's performance was overshadowed by Steve Waugh, who scored an unbeaten 202 and 60 not out in a drawn match that also saw Matthew Elliott notch a century. However, the result meant little when compared with the off-field happenings. By early November, the vast majority of Australia's first-class cricketers had signed a petition that gave the ACA the authority to call a strike. Thankfully, the following months led to compromises between the ACA and the ACB. There were no strikes, and by September 1998 both parties signed an agreement that would boost the payment to each State squad by $300 000. Some of Australia's most senior players were forced to take pay cuts under the restructure, but the ACA had achieved its aim of lifting the income of the average Australian first-class cricketer.

The 1997–98 season also proved a profitable summer for Shane on the field. It was a season in which individual performances outshone team efforts. Under new coach Steve Small, NSW finished fourth in the Sheffield Shield and runners-up to Queensland in the Mercantile Mutual Cup. Although he was once again overlooked by Australia's selectors, Shane continued to demonstrate his talent with his highest first-class score, an unbeaten 183 in the 10-wicket win by the Blues against South Australia at the Adelaide Oval. It was the last match before Christmas, a crucial one for Shane because he'd been told the day before the game that his position was in jeopardy — if he failed against the Redbacks he'd be staring at a stint in the State Second XI. But any thoughts of dumping him were lost in the trail of balls that bounced back from the Adelaide Oval's boundary fence. He hit 20 fours and three sixes off just 206 balls. It was the highlight of his summer, which yielded 570 runs at 47.5 and 12 wickets at 48.67 in 10 matches. His batting also left an impression in the Mercantile Mutual Cup series. In eight games he tallied 214 runs at an average of 30.57, and a strike rate of 96.83. He was at his most brutal when the Blues savaged Western Australia by 98 runs in Perth. Shane blasted 99 not out from just 79 balls, including eight fours and a six. Shane recalls:

Any good score could help me get back into the Australian team. It was so tough being on the outer. After being given another little taste on the Ashes tour, I just wanted to be back with the big guys. But I tried not to dwell on it. I began convincing myself that it was just a fact of life. The bottom line was that I wasn't performing consistently, and I could only blame myself. Everyone has an unlucky run sooner or later. When it happens some guys bag the selectors, others worry about their captain not giving them a go. To be honest, that's all bullshit. You make your own luck. It's as simple as that. And that's the philosophy I started to take.

There were times during the season that I hoped for a recall, but I was determined not to let it worry me.

The closest Shane came to a recall during the season was in Adelaide when he played for Australia against an invitation Academy team to celebrate the Academy's tenth anniversary. He was dismissed for 0. It was a forgettable score, but a memorable dismissal: he was caught and bowled Brett Lee!

Shane may have been an outsider during the '97–98 season, but a controversial shift in selection policy gave him added hope for the future. The ACB split the Test and limited-overs teams, a decision which saw the dumping of Mark Taylor and Ian Healy. Steve Waugh took over the captaincy of the one-day games, while Taylor remained in charge of the Test side. Arguments raged on both sides of the boundary. Shane remembers:

Not being in the team at the time meant I wasn't as close to the issue as the players on the inside. But I do think it was a good idea to have separate sides. One-day cricket was changing, and we had to keep up with the times. The Sri Lankans led the way at the '96 World Cup by being really aggressive at the start of their innings. We were still using the approach of building a solid foundation at the top which hopefully left the way for the middle order to go for the quick runs. But it wasn't working, so something had to be done. When Adam Gilchrist began opening with Mark Waugh, Australia's batting went to a different level. It was the start of the shift towards having more all-rounders in the team. If the top order made a good start, it made sense to have big hitters in the middle order so they could have a swing in the final overs. And many of the best hitters in Australia are all blokes who can bat and bowl as well.

When the split first happened I didn't think too much about my chances, but in hindsight it's fair to say it helped my cause.

CHAPTER EIGHT

MIRROR IMAGES

There was one day when Brett, Grant and I were looking through some of Shane's Australian gear at the Lees' home. There were shirts, tracksuit pants, and a helmet. I suggested to Brett: 'Why don't you try the helmet on and see if it fits you.' But he shook his head and said, 'No way. You have to earn that. I'll never put an Australian one on unless it's my own.'

Adam Rainford

By the end of the 1995–96 season, having recovered from his back injury, Brett felt as though he had to begin all over again. During his recuperation in Mount Warrigal, Brett spent long hours in the family garage walking through the final three paces of his delivery, and analysing them in an old mirror taken from a wardrobe. It was a technique used by Dennis Lillee many years earlier: 'It was something I did when we didn't have regular access to videos,' recalls Lillee. 'It was the easiest way to see how my action was going. It was a good little tool because it gave me instant feedback. I suggested Brett do it as well.'

His injury was proof that he had to change his mixed action. The remodelling process continued when he was invited back for a second stint at the Australian Cricket Academy from April 1996. Under the guidance of fast-bowling coach Richard Done, he slowly modified his body angles at the point of delivery:

I had always bowled chest on, but was always trying to look through the window over my left shoulder. But by doing that, my head was falling away and I was hyperextending. So Richard worked on me looking through my left arm, which did help me, but it was slow work. I wasn't really strong through the chest and shoulders, and when I became tired I went back to the old habits of twisting the lower back. At the time I didn't appreciate how much work I had to do, and it wasn't until I did my back again two years later that I fully realised how important the changes were.

It probably sounds strange, but I spent nearly as much time on my batting as my bowling at the Academy. When I first arrived at the Academy in '95 I was a true tailender, and Rod Marsh started helping me with my batting. At Campbelltown, I always used to charge the first ball I faced because being a number 11 I tried to think like an opposing bowler. I figured when I came into bat and took guard on leg-stump, the bowler would see all three stumps and obviously think the best way to get me out was to try to york me. So my theory was simple: If I charged the ball I could make it into a full toss and hit it back over the bowler's head! Nine times out of ten it worked until the Channel Nine program 'A Current Affair' did a story on Shane, Grant and me playing backyard cricket. During the interview, Shane let the cat out of the bag about my tactics, and from then on it seemed every first ball I got in grade was up around my head! So I got into the habit of just slogging madly because I never knew where the ball was going to pitch. Sometimes I'd jag 15 or 20 runs, but most of the time I was on my way back within a couple of balls.

When I went to the Academy I still thought I had to keep slogging, but Rod Marsh's advice was simple and straight to the point. He said no team wanted a player who couldn't hold a bat at all, and if it came to the stage where selectors had to choose between two bowlers of similar ability, they'd always give the nod to the better batsman.

There were heaps of days when Rod just fed me balls, or I'd do extra sessions of 'throw downs' with a mate. It was the first time in my life that I'd really worked on my batting. All the training helped me when I played second grade for Mosman as a batsman at the end of the '95–96 season, and by the time I returned to the Academy I was determined to make more progress. My aim was to continually improve my position in the lower order. There's no point ever being totally happy with what you've achieved; you should always look higher, and that's the way I began to treat my batting.

The Academy was a fantastic experience. I'd barely met any of the other players when I arrived for my first stint in '95, but within a week we were all good mates. And the same thing happened in '96. Rod Marsh was very supportive and full of encouragement, but he was also hard and very, very honest. That's what you need in a coach: someone who'll kick you up the backside if you do the wrong thing. He was always very straight, unlike some coaches who'll tell players what they want to hear but never fix their faults. Rod left a big impression on me, and his influence made me even more determined to represent Australia. The injury had been a setback but, after having no problems in my second stint at the Academy, I was keen to return home and make up for lost time by starting the '96–97 season with a bang. All I wanted to do was bowl fast for Mosman, and hopefully get noticed by State selectors. Shane's selection in the Australian team was also a big motivator. His debut came during the time that I had my back injury. At that stage I was really beginning to think about where I was going in life. I wasn't working and wasn't playing cricket. Should I do a TAFE course? Or pick up some other work? What was going to make me happy? Seeing Shane smashing the West Indies on debut left me in no doubt. I just wanted to play cricket for Australia.

Phil Emery, former NSW captain and wicket-keeper, remembers:

We were playing a warm-up game at Drummoyne Oval when the rain came down and forced the team to have an indoor session at the SCG.

Brett was there training with the Colts. Last ball I faced from him, he ran through the crease, bounced me, and hit me in the hand. I blew up! My arm was numb, I couldn't feel my elbow. He came up to me to see if I was all right, but I threw the bat at him and shouted, 'I don't care what you do during a game, but don't take a cheap shot at me in the nets, you dickhead!' He apologised and said, 'Oh, I suppose you're OK then.'

Shane came up to me and asked if I'd had a go at his brother. When I said I had, Shane replied, 'Yeh, you should have too because Brett knows where every ball is going.'

I suppose he was out just trying to impress.

It wasn't hard for Brett to leave lasting impressions with any batsman he bowled to, but it took some time to alert State selectors that he'd fully recovered from the back injury that wrecked his 1995–96 season. Although in a hurry to make up for lost time, he was forced to wait in the wings during his comeback in '96–97. Although he played for the NSW Second XI, he failed to earn a call-up to the first-class ranks. Much of his season was spent grinding out the overs for Mosman. He finished second in the first-grade aggregates, taking 29 wickets at 20.28. More importantly, there were no signs of back problems. Brett recalls:

I felt great. I was really keen to get into the Sheffield Shield team, but I knew I had to wait my turn. The '96–97 season taught me much about patience. Before my back injury I was on a roll, playing different junior representative matches all the time, but in '96–97 I had to go back a few steps and start again. I suppose I was always in too much of a hurry to get to the next level, so that season ended up being a great learning experience that showed me how hard I'd have to work to make it in the senior game. It was a real challenge.

It wasn't until the following season that his patience was rewarded. After warming up for the season in South Africa on a tour with the Academy Brett resumed playing grade, and by late November he was selected ahead of fellow rookie Stuart Clark to make his Sheffield Shield debut against Western Australia at the SCG. What followed during the four-day match led to one of the most remarkable wins by a NSW team in recent history. The Blues trailed by 223 runs on the first innings, but ensured a dramatic finish when their second innings total of 5 declared for 477 left the Warriors a final-day target of 255. The visitors were dismissed for 194 with just 12 balls remaining. Brett was the central figure in the nerve-racking final overs:

My first memory of that match is the buzz I got when I walked out onto the field for the first time. I was right behind Shane. I'd walked out in front or behind him quite a few times in grade matches, but this was for NSW. This was the real thing. It was great to have the Baggy Blue on.

It was a funny sort of game. We were up against it after Western Australia took the first innings lead. They might have made a big score, but I was quite happy with the way I bowled. I took 1–99 and wasn't as nervous as I thought I'd be. But my heart was thumping when Phil Emery threw me the ball at the death in the second innings. We needed to get three wickets in the last few overs. I bowled Jamie Stewart for a duck, then MacGilla (Stuart MacGill) got Matthew Garnaut. One wicket to go! Brett Mulder and Brendon Julian survived an over, which meant we only had three to go, two to be bowled by me. A few of the blokes in the team came up to me and said, 'Come on, you gotta do it.' It was only then that I thought, 'Shit, you guys have thrown me in the deep end here.' I was getting pretty edgy, but I was lucky. Midway through the over BJ turned the strike around, and I had a chance at Mulder. With my last ball he played all over a yorker and was bowled. All of a sudden everyone came up and started hugging me. It was actually one of the biggest thrills, and biggest wins of my life.

Emery never considered it a gamble to call on his debutante at such a critical time:

I copped a bit of flak from the commentators for bringing Brett back on when I did, but I knew this kid was so quick and accurate that he was going to be a real handful for the tailenders to keep out. He'd earlier hit Tom Moody in the head. He terrorised him, and really took it to him. That further proved to me that he wouldn't back down to anyone.

He didn't let us down in those final couple of overs. I've seen tailenders bugger up many sides because they just block, but when you have a bloke like Brett who's seriously quick and has no problem pinning any batsman in the head, you have to use him whenever you can. Plus on that day he was getting so much reverse swing, the tailenders were always going to be in trouble.

The praise from Brett's team-mates was widespread. No-one argued that his stunning contribution was a sure sign of what would happen in the future.

Former NSW spinner David Freedman says:

The win was the best game I've ever been associated with. I took three wickets in the second innings. I still remember it vividly. It was a wonderful game. It was early in the season; we'd struggled the year before, and were struggling again, and this was our first win for some time. Brett played a very big role. He bowled really, really quickly: big inswinging yorkers that any top-order batsman would have had trouble playing. It was a much tougher ask for the tail. It was a big call to put the pressure on him in the final overs after the spinners had done most of the work all day, but he stepped up and bowled great. You could tell that to make that sort of mark on his debut, he was destined to play a special role in the future. He had the world at his feet.

In just one Shield match Brett had made an impact that spread far beyond the SCG. As happens on the cricket grapevine, word quickly spread through the first-class ranks that the brother of Shane Lee was a player to be watched. The Warriors returned home saying that the Blues had perhaps discovered the fastest bowler in Australia. Anyone who could make a ball climb suddenly to Tom Moody's towering heights on the slowest pitch in Australia was something out of the ordinary. Brett, who had turned 21 a fortnight before his Shield debut, had come of age.

A month later, national selectors confirmed Brett was on the fast track to higher honours when the Australia 'A' team was chosen to play South Africa in a four-day game at the Gabba. It was a formidable side boasting Michael Slater, Justin Langer, Adam Gilchrist, Michael Bevan, and Stuart MacGill. However, no name created as much interest as Brett Lee, who'd been chosen after playing just one Shield match. Brett laughs:

Looking back, it's still hard to believe that I got such a quick call-up. When I heard who else was in the 'A' team, I had to shake myself. Guys like Slats and Bevo were hardened Test cricketers. And here I was playing with them. In some ways I felt like I didn't belong. There was so much experience in the team. Stuart Law was captain, and he'd been around a lot, and I was determined not to disappoint him. There'd been a bit of talk about me in the papers, but apart from that many of the guys in the team didn't know much about me. I was Shane Lee's brother. That was about as far as my reputation went.

But I'd been given the biggest opportunity of my career, so I wasn't going to let it go. I suppose I had to prove things to a few different people. I had to prove to my new team-mates that I deserved my place, and wasn't being given an easy ride. I had to give something back to the selectors who'd shown their faith in me, and I also had to prove to myself that I could make another step up. Plus, I wanted to make sure that the South Africans finished the match thinking that they'd see a lot more of me in the future. I was really pumped to do well for so many reasons, but nothing turned out the way I'd planned. I took two wickets for the match, and again wrecked my back.

When I watched footage from that match, I could see I was trying to bowl too quickly. As a result, my action was falling away heaps and there were lots of counter-rotations making my body twist awkwardly. In that game, I actually got heat stroke because it was forty plus degrees in the middle. A combination of trying to bowl too fast, having a mixed action, and being so exhausted from the heat led to my stress fractures reopening again. I was shattered. I'd worked so hard to come back from my last injury, but now I was back where I started.

But this time the recovery was much tougher because I was put in a brace for more than three months. It went from my head to my bum, I looked like Frankenstein, and was basically off my feet for 14 weeks. I lost heaps of fitness and muscle strength. It was very frustrating wearing the brace because I'm the type of person who likes to be doing things all the time. But I was in this brace for nearly 24 hours a day, only taking it off to have a shower. It was the most frustrating period I've ever been through. Not only did I have to worry about the injury, but I was angry that the injury had come at a time when I was just starting to make an impression in the senior game. There was so much I wanted to do, but just couldn't. The rest of the season was a write off.

Adam Rainford recalls how difficult the period was for his best mate:

It was a scary time for Brett. He kept thinking positively, and told everyone he was going to play again no matter what. He always remained confident, but there were times when he admitted to me that he was really worried about what could happen. At the back of his mind he was wondering if he would ever play again. But his strength of character got him through.

There were some funny sides to come out of it all. Brett loved going out, but he was conscious of what other people would think. So, he'd wear two shirts over the brace to try to cover it up. All his close mates used to laugh and sledge him because he looked like a Ken doll. He was really stiff and his movement was pretty limited. But he got used to it.

The injury confirmed the need for Brett to change his action. Although he had worked on slight alterations after his first back problem, it wasn't until his second setback that he realised his longevity as a fast bowler depended on some critical rebuilding. After he was allowed out of the brace, he started the slow grind back to full fitness. And once he was able to bowl again during the 1998 winter, he called on his mentor, Dennis Lillee.

Lillee remembers:

At first the process meant looking at lots of videos. We had to make sure he understood where he was going wrong mechanically. The process was simple for me, but it can be bloody difficult to explain it to a young player. By experimenting with a few different actions in front of the video camera, we came up with a different action. Brett simply had to bowl front on. Until that point, the top half of his body was front on, but the bottom half was partly side on. We had to work hard on getting his feet as straight on as possible to prevent counter-rotation.

Brett started by walking through his new action before he started to bowl with it. The period was over months and months and months. There was no quick fix to the process, but he took it all on board. At the same time we spoke about the need for more body strength and flexibility, particularly in the core muscle group. You don't need the 'beach look' to bowl fast, but you need good core strength. And Brett threw himself headlong into that with special weight training and flexibility exercises. He worked very hard, and it was amazing how much he had improved the next time I saw him, just before the new season started. He was a much more impressive guy who bowled what we call 'fairly safely'. You're never totally safe when you're a fast bowler.

Brett used the mirror technique to further consolidate his new action. At first he took just three steps, then five, and slowly he worked back to his full run-up. He was stronger, fitter, and more determined than he'd ever been. Surely nothing could go wrong as he prepared for the 1998–99 season.

CHAPTER NINE

KEEPING THE SEAM STRAIGHT

*There's a lot of similarities between selling and playing
cricket. In selling, you've gotta be part of a team.
When a customer comes in, it becomes a challenge,
just like a batsman coming out to bat. You have to try
to work him out, try to pick out his weakness, then you
try to nail him. I just love selling suits. It's a reality check
for me. It teaches me new skills, and I meet new people.
What a great job.*

Brett Lee

Not all was going against Brett at the time of his second back injury. Six months earlier, a surprise phone call from the owner of Barclays Menswear in Sydney changed Brett's outlook on life. Richard Bowman had been in the clothing business for nearly 20 years, continuing a four-decade-long family tradition. He'd first met Brett in 1995 when fitting out Australia's Under-19 players with team blazers. Who was to know what an impact that meeting would have.

Bowman remembers:

My first impression of Brett was to think how well-mannered and adjusted he was. I didn't know at that stage he was such a good cricketer. But he certainly left an impression on me. Around the same time I employed a young rugby union player, Tom Bowman, who was no relation. He soon went into the State squad, and I was happy to give him as much time off as he needed for training and playing commitments. But it did mean I had a hole to fill in the staff. I needed to find someone who would complement Tom's role, so I thought that the next time I went to measure some teams I'd start looking. But then I remembered and thought, 'Hold on a minute. I don't have to look because I met this boy with the Australian Under-19s.'

So I thought I'd ring Brett Lee and see what he was doing. I first rang the NSW Cricket Association. They were reluctant to give any phone number out, but when I told them I wanted to give Brett a job as a suit salesman they gave it to me straight away.

When I rang Brett up I introduced myself, but there was no need because he actually remembered who I was. I asked him if he was working, and he said he was just doing a bit of cricket coaching but had nothing permanent. So, I invited him in to talk to me if he was interested. The next day he came into my office, and was met by my colleague, Melissa Barbaresco. He'd made a real effort. He had a pretty shocking suit on and a pretty shocking shirt, but he'd made an effort. He was very nervous because he was dripping with sweat and rain, but I could tell he really wanted this to work out.

I asked him what he wanted to do with his life, and he replied that he hoped to make something out of cricket but wasn't 100 per cent sure because of his back. He was keen to have a go at what I had to offer, so the next day he went on a trip with Melissa to the Bulli Harness Racing Club to arrange a small order of uniforms. Melissa returned full of praise, saying that Brett was a natural. He liked people, and they liked him. So I made the decision on the spot to employ him. It all started from there.

We first taught him all about sizes, fittings, fabrics, and techniques. He just fell straight into it. He loved clothes, and I allowed him to dress in our suits and shirts. That was the beginning of the walking public relations machine.

Early on in the piece I remember him saying to me after someone had spoken poorly to him: 'My mother told me never to talk down to anybody.' They were pretty mature words for someone so young.

In the past few years he has made a significant difference to our business. Obviously it works both ways. I gave Thomas and Brett a chance, but they also helped me. If you can combine sporting aspirations with commercial aspirations, you have an edge. And that's how I've tried to help Brett and Thomas. Tom started it, but Brett perfected it. The coverage he has given the business has been fantastic. We had a strong business, but I was aware in non-branded stores that we needed to move the image, and Brett was perfect. He became our own international public relations dream.

The conversations between Brett and the customers can be amazing. Brett was back in the store the morning after the Sydney Test against India had finished. Two customers in the shop couldn't believe it was him, so one whispered to the other, 'Is that Brett Lee?' Finally they asked Brett, who nodded and said, 'Yes.' The two men couldn't believe it. 'What are you doing here? You were on TV yesterday playing for Australia.' Brett simply replied, 'Yeh, but I was working here before I did that. I love this job.' They were just stunned. I was just sitting back watching and thinking, 'This really works.'

People want to be served by Brett. You have these normally reserved men who come into the shop being incredibly friendly and asking questions while being fitted for a suit. Conversations go something like this:

'Congratulations on the game.'

'Thanks very much. Do you like the sky blue or the dark blue?'

'What's it like bowling so fast?'

'I love it, but it's hard work. Do you want cuffs or no cuffs with the trousers?'

'Cuffs, please.'

'You know fast bowling is all about getting into a rhythm.'

By this stage Brett is down on his knees pinning up the legs of trousers. Before you know it the suit is sold, and we have a happy customer who not only has a suit, but got a real kick out of being served by Brett Lee.

Schoolgirls go nuts over him. He gets fan mail addressed to the shop, girls come in, and once we had a mini-riot out the front of the shop. The entrance to Centrepoint Tower is on the same level as the shop, and there was this group of schoolgirls who'd just come down. One of them saw Brett, then the next thing you know there were 40 girls out the front of the shop screaming and carrying on, asking for autographs and just hoping to catch a glimpse of Brett. They were screaming and pleading, 'Come out Brett, please come out and talk to us.' The teacher had to come in and try to literally marshall her troops away, but they wouldn't go. So Brett came out and signed a few autographs and spoke to the girls. I was at the other end of Centrepoint, and when I heard the noise I immediately thought that there had to be a pop star somewhere. It was weird. I can understand how young girls adore him. He's just so clean and keen. So pure.

Before he made it to his current status, I actually hadn't seen him bowl, so I went out with my wife and watched him play a bit of grade cricket. After seeing him bowl I realised he wasn't just the average cricketer. But the beauty is that he's still the same kid that he's always been. It's as though he's still playing grade cricket. He's the same way in the shop.

Long-term, Barclays will see less of him and maybe one day he'll want to run his own clothing business, but he needs to be prepared for when he does hang his hat somewhere outside of cricket. It takes brains. And Brett has the brains to do it. And hopefully I've helped him with the grounding.

He will always have a career in business after cricket. Whether it be rubber goods, real estate, clothing, you name it, he has a career in business. All he is doing now is sowing the seeds for other opportunities after cricket. Brett has to maximise his opportunities while he can. It's all about balance. There's a big column and a little column. Cricket is the big column, but you need to have the little columns to keep the feet on the ground. When Brett comes back off tour he still needs to look after his balance, and there will always be a chance for him to come into this store and spend some time in the little column.

Brett is of the opinion that work is good for him. Wherever he goes I wish him the best success. Talent and humility aren't often mixed together in the same quantity that Brett has them. It's been a pleasure helping him.

Perhaps Brett was always destined to play a role in the fashion industry. Helen Lee acknowledges all three of her sons have long been 'clothes horses'. Brett too admits the fit was snug:

It was Sunday afternoon when Richard contacted me at Shane's place. I remembered straight away who he was because he'd seemed the nicest person when I'd first met him a few years earlier. He was straight to the point, and when he said he had a position going for a suit salesman, I got pretty excited. I was looking for work, so the offer couldn't have come at a better time.

I was invited in the very next day. I was still living at Mount Warrigal at that stage, so I had to leave home nice and early. And although I gave myself plenty of time, I started panicking when I couldn't find a car spot in the city. It was pouring with rain, and when I finally found a park I had to sprint through a few streets before I got undercover. By the time I walked into Barclays I was soaking wet and shaking with nerves. I must have looked really bad.

But Richard was extremely friendly. He sat me down and basically said, 'We haven't seen you sell, but you can start tomorrow.' I went down to Bulli with Melissa on the Tuesday; then on the Wednesday I was thrown in the deep end when the day's first customer arrived at about ten past nine. The customer told me he wanted to try on a three-button, single-breasted suit with a notch lapel in a Prince of Wales check. I had no idea, so I said, 'I think some new stock has just come in, so I'll just go and get someone to help you.' Richard helped me out, but it was hard to hide my nerves. It was so new and different to anything I'd done before. After about three days I was getting the hang of it. It was probably a bit like getting my first wicket in a new grade. Once I got one, I had a bit of confidence. And the same thing went for suit selling. Once I'd sold a couple, I was much more relaxed and comfortable. As soon as a customer came in I'd nearly go straight for the neck with a tape measure. I suppose it would have looked pretty funny from an outsider's view because I was just so keen to impress and do a good job. I'd been given a fantastic opportunity, and really wanted to make it work.

The first few months were pretty hard because I was travelling from Mount Warrigal every day. I would drive the hour and half up to Sydney, then leave my car at the Domain car park. It cost me $15 a day plus petrol, so when I took all the expenses out I wasn't actually making that much. But I wasn't going to chuck it in.

By the time cricket season came around, I had the added weight of fitting in training. I'd be up by 6.30 in the morning, and on Tuesdays and Thursdays I'd leave work early and go out to the SCG. I wouldn't get home until about 9.30 at night. After a few months I was pretty well worn out.

Not long after my twenty-first birthday I eventually moved up to Sydney, and all the travel was no longer a worry. I shared a flat with NSW opener Rod Davison near the city, and the walk to work took 20 minutes each way. It was much more relaxing and I began to save a bit more money.

But I wasn't in it for the dollars, I was after the experience. At first it was very hard for me to take money from customers, but I knew if I didn't then my life as a salesman would be very, very short! Now I look at it as though I'm not taking money from a customer, but I'm giving them a service. They're paying for a good suit, and need to be looked after properly. That's where I fit in.

I've always loved fashion, and since I started at Barclays there've been very few days when it has been hard to get up, get dressed in a suit, and get going. Richard taught me you can't achieve anything by staying in bed all day. He has had a big influence on me; we've become good mates, and he gave me the confidence and help to launch my own label last May. Since I started as a suit salesman, I'd always thought I'd love to bring out my own clothing label. Because of the close relationship with Richard, Barclays became the perfect place to launch it.

Richard and I sat down, did some figures, and decided we'd go for it. I was after smart casual wear, weekend wear, good-fitting clothing — the type I like wearing. Richard was full of encouragement, so we've decided to test the water and see what happens. We couldn't call it Lee because of Lee jeans, and we decided not to name it Binga because few people would know who Binga is. So we settled on something nice and simple. The Brett Lee label has only just started, but hopefully after cricket finishes I'd like to really become involved in the industry, and even design a few clothes myself. It's an exciting opportunity.

And to think it all came from a totally unexpected phone call.

CHAPTER TEN

ON THE COMEBACK TRAIL

*Shane has always been a great mimicker.
We'd name a bowler at training, and it would be up
to Shane to put on the act: 'Come on, give us a
Greg Matthews.' He'd go back, flick the hair, wiggle
the bum, then come in and give a near perfect
impersonation. He was super talented. Everything
looked easy for him.*

David Freedman

Shane may have been a successful role player at NSW training sessions, but as the 1998–99 season began he was still trying to discover how far his own character could take him. After two years in the international wilderness, he knew this season was a critical one in his career. The World Cup in England was just eight months away, and if Shane was to earn a berth every game during the home summer could help boost his chances. However, if he failed and again missed out on Australian selection, he feared he would drift into the domain of those players who'd made the top level but were seemingly forgotten no sooner than they had been discovered. This season wasn't only going to be a test of talent, but one of mental strength.

His challenge began badly in the Blues' Mercantile Mutual Cup opener against Queensland at North Sydney Oval. In a modest team score of 8–231, Shane was trapped lbw by Brendan Creevey for a duck. NSW restricted their rivals to 9–228, but Shane wasn't called on to bowl by captain Phil Emery.

Two weeks later he bowled just nine overs without taking a wicket when the Blues launched their Sheffield Shield campaign with a first-innings loss to South Australia at the Adelaide Oval. However, his batting returned to its powerful best in an unbeaten innings of 102. It was one of the most polished displays of Shane's career, a shining contrast to his bowling, that prompted respected journalist Phil Wilkins (*Sydney Morning Herald*, 23 October 1998) to write:

> Lee, 25, is a powerful figure, but his pace bowling is unfortunately lowering in value as evidenced by the nine overs skipper Phil Emery gave him in SA's first innings of 108 overs.
>
> Perhaps that is how Lee's game will evolve, a fine batsman and capable international whose bowling fell short of making him the essential all-rounder for next year's World Cup and, worse, failing to win a Test cap. It will be a sorry day.

The fluctuating start to the season continued when Shane fell for 4 and a golden duck, and took 1–30 off 10 overs as NSW slumped to an innings defeat against Queensland in a Shield match that was transferred to Canberra's Manuka Oval because of the poor state of the outfield at the SCG. At times the match was played in bitterly cold conditions; many players had to wear at least two jumpers in the field, and the usually frowned-upon habit of putting hands in pockets was a necessity between deliveries. A day after the game finished, Shane discovered there was a much more enjoyable way to fill his pockets during the Mercantile Mutual Cup match against

Canberra when he lofted a drive into a specially placed jackpot sign at the long-on boundary. It netted him $90 000.

Shane remembers:

We'd been sent in to bat and lost a couple of early wickets and were struggling a bit. But then Rod Davison and I put our heads down and got us into a pretty good position. It was just one of those days when I was timing the ball really well right from the start of the innings. I was feeling pretty confident and was really keen to get among them. The Shield match against Queensland had been really disappointing for me, so I was determined to make up for it. But I didn't expect to make such a big profit out of it! All-rounder Ian Garrity came on to bowl, and he put one right up in the slot for me to have a go at. As soon as I hit the ball I knew it was going to smack into the sign. I watched it all the way until a big clunk was music to my ears.

Rod and I did high-fives, then I signalled to my team-mates that I'd be sharing the money with them. Steve Waugh was the only other batsman to have hit the bull's eye, in a game against Western Australia in 1994. He won $140 000, and devised a formula that allowed all the team to have a slice of the money. My initial plan was to take all the guys away to Hawaii because we'd been having a rough time, and a trip away would be good for morale. But it didn't eventuate. A few guys just wanted their share of the money. It annoyed me a bit because as the saying goes, 'You never look a gift-horse in the mouth'. It was something we never had to begin with, and I thought it would have been good for the whole squad. Yeh, I was pissed off.

I ended up getting 85 in the game, Rod made 89, and we went on to win by 30 runs. It might sound strange, but I always knew I would hit one of the signs sooner or later. And I reckon one day I'll hit another one. I'm pretty arsey like that!

But good fortune didn't lead to consistency. After scoring 67 and 65 in the Sheffield Shield match a week later against Victoria in Melbourne, Shane fell for a duck in the Mercantile Mutual Cup encounter against the Bushrangers.

Despite his unpredictable form, he batted well enough to reach 483 Shield runs at an average of 48.3 by Christmas. His bowling was less rewarding. Used sparingly for just 68 overs, he claimed 5 wickets. His limited-overs statistics were also dominated by the bat: 174 runs at 43.5, but not one wicket.

However, selectors saw behind the figures and decided their richly talented all-rounder deserved a recall for Australia's World Series campaign against England and Sri Lanka.

Shane says:

I was relieved to be back in the squad. But that relief was matched by pressure. It was only when I got back with the players that I realised how much I'd missed during the last two years. For the first time I knew playing cricket was what I wanted to do with my life. But I didn't want to treat it as a career because if I looked at it in that way, I looked at it as earning money, and then I was taking away the essence of what it's all about. I would have played for nothing that season because I was just so excited to be back. It means everything to represent your country, and it's something I remain very passionate about.

I knew it wasn't going to be easy to stay in the side, but I was a bit wiser than when I was first picked. The selectors had shown faith in me, now it was my turn to show faith in myself. Unlike my previous stint with the team, I wasn't going to think too far ahead. But that was hard to do because the World Cup wasn't that far away. I just kept telling myself to forget about it, and I simply tried to concentrate on doing my best one game at a time. You hear nearly every sportsman say that, but it's so true. If you start jumping too far ahead, you lose sight of what you should be concentrating on.

The approach worked. In his first game back, Shane scored 18 off 21 balls in Australia's three-wicket loss to the Sri Lankans in Hobart. For the remainder of the series his strike rate hovered at nearly a run a ball, a difficult but imperative target for a batsman who inevitably came to the crease with just a handful of overs remaining in most innings. His highest score for the tournament was 41 off 53 deliveries in Australia's 16-run win over England under lights at the Adelaide Oval. His aggression was no better illustrated than in the second final against England at the MCG when he slammed 20 off just 9 balls as Australia cruised to victory to claim its twelfth domestic limited-overs crown.

Despite all Shane achieved with the bat in the series, it was one of his bowling performances during Australia's 43-run win over Sri Lanka that stood out. Shane says:

It was the last game before the finals, a day/nighter in Melbourne and thanks to Gilly [Adam Gilchrist] we made 8–310. Gilly was unbelievable. He started smashing as soon as he went in, and he just kept on going. It was one of the most incredible innings I've ever seen because he rarely played a bad shot, and was hitting the bowlers so hard that there were times when the fieldsman were wringing their hands if they stopped a ball. He made 154 off 129 balls, and I was really glad I wasn't out there bowling. When you have a batsman as talented as Gilly, in that sort of mood, it can be pretty embarrassing for any bowler. You can let the ball go and think, 'Yeh, that's not a bad one,' then all of a sudden it's flying back over your head and into the crowd.

Up until that point in the series, my longest bowling spell had been six overs. I'd taken a couple of wickets, and was happy enough with the way the ball was coming out, but I knew I could do better. Because they were chasing such a big score the Sri Lankans threw the bat at everything from the start. They were really firing, and were ahead of the run rate. I came on around the twentieth over, and it just turned out to be my lucky day. I got a lot of bounce from the start, which always helps against subcontinent batsmen. They're so used to lower and slower wickets that they can get into a fair bit of trouble on bouncier decks. Four wickets fell in five overs, and we put the screws on. I finished with 5–33 off 8.1 overs, and was happiest about picking up Aravinda de Silva and Arjuna Ranatunga in the one over. Especially Ranatunga. He can be a really irritating bloke to play against, but you have to admire his fight. Once he edged one to Gilly, we thought we could control them.

It was my first five-wicket haul, and although I was pleased there was no doubt who the player of the match was. Gilly deserved it; I'll remember his innings for a long time.

In all, Shane took 8 wickets at 24.75, and tallied 146 runs at 24.33 for the series. He returned to help NSW into the Mercantile Mutual Cup Final against Victoria, but it wasn't a memorable match for either himself or his team-mates. The Bushrangers won by 39 runs. Shane was dismissed for 9 and took 1–32 off 5.3 overs.

It was a much tougher Shield season for NSW, finishing last on the table after claiming just one outright win. Shane's return showed the sharp contrast between his batting and bowling fortunes: 602 runs at 50.17, and 6 wickets at 57.67. However, nothing could discredit his eye-catching displays in the international arena. He'd been one of the form players of the summer. While his domestic season was over, the hard work was just about to begin.

★ ★ ★

For the many thousands of tourists who visit the enchanting islands of the Caribbean every year, there's little reason to think beyond sand, palm trees, tans, rum cocktails, steel drums, and limbo dancing. In Antigua, the locals boast they have a beach for every day of the year; while in Trinidad, hips and feet shuffle and sway to music that is not only on the streets, but also in the imagination. In Barbados, elderly women dress in their Sunday best every day of the week, and Jamaicans say they gave the world one of its greatest gifts ... reggae! To the visitor, the West Indian way of life can prove as enticing and palatable as the delicious curried goat rotis that Bridgetown's street vendors make with a smile and a laugh.

However, to a professional cricketer, a trip to the Caribbean can sometimes leave a bitter taste in the mouth. And so it proved during parts of Australia's 1999 tour. It was the start of a new era:

Mark Taylor had retired, leaving Steve Waugh to assume the Test captaincy in addition to his limited-overs responsibilities. Following a 2–2 draw in the Tests, the Australians reshuffled their squad for a seven-match one-day series, the last chance for Waugh and his 14 team-mates to finetune before heading to England for the World Cup. After his successful home summer, Shane was a certain selection. He couldn't find touch with the bat in the early matches, but showed glimpses of his best when he scored 19 not out and 47 in the final two encounters. His best return with the ball was 2–26 off 6.2 overs in the fourth game at the picturesque Queen's Park in Port of Spain, Trinidad. However, individual performances throughout the series were overshadowed by ugly crowd disturbances that tainted two of the last three games.

Shane recalls:

I was rested from Game Five in Georgetown, Guyana and in hindsight it was a pretty good game to have off. The result came down to the last ball. Steve Waugh was facing part-time spinner Keith Arthurton, and Shane Warne was at the other end. They needed four to win. It was pretty tense everywhere. The crowd were yelling and screaming, but we were all pretty quiet in the dressing room. Tugga [Steve Waugh] hit the ball through mid-wicket, and before you knew it the crowds were sprinting onto the field. Tugga and Warney somehow tried to steal a third run to tie the game. By this time Arthurton had the ball back and was looking for a stump to run Tugga out, but all six stumps had been stolen by the crowd.

We were confused in the dressing room. When the third run was made most of us thought we could claim it, but no-one seemed sure. A few of the boys were giving high-fives, but we were mostly waiting for Tugga and Warney to get off the field to find out what was happening. By the time they did, the fans were abusing us. Tugga and our manager, Steve Bernard, went into an inquiry with the match referee, Raman Subba Row, and when they returned they told us that the match was going to be declared a tie. There were still hundreds of angry fans outside the dressing room yelling and screaming abuse at us. At this stage we were wondering how the hell we were going to get to our team bus. Some security guards came in and told us that they weren't going to announce the game over the PA because there could be a riot, and for the moment we had to stay where we were because they were worried for our safety if we moved. We must have waited in the dressing room for an hour and a half before the security guys rushed us out a side door and onto the bus. Thankfully we made our way out of there with no real problems, but most of us were still pretty worried until we got back to the hotel. It's that sort of incident that makes you realise it would only take one idiot to cause a really serious accident. Tugga told the media that it was only a matter of time before a player was attacked like Monica Seles was. It was a pretty strong call to make, but all of us believed him.

We all hoped nothing worse would follow in the final two games, but in the last match in Bridgetown a tangle between Brendon Julian and hometown hero Sherwin Campbell nearly started World War Three. The West Indies were chasing 253 to win the game and tie the series. BJ was bowling when Sherwin went for a quick single. The two collided in the middle of the pitch, Sherwin was on his backside and was easily run out.

As soon as it happened I thought, 'Yeh, go on, you're out.' A few of the boys gave Sherwin a bit of a sendoff, but Sherwin started protesting. And as soon as he did that, the crowd started booing and throwing anything they could find onto the field. I was out on the point fence in front of the scoreboard, and glass bottles were clearing my head and flying on both sides of me. I thought to myself, 'This is bullshit. I'm not fielding here. I'll go and field in the ring, but not out here. It's a matter of time before I cop something.' By that stage Tugga was calling the team into the middle. When we were all in a huddle, he said, 'We're not staying out here, guys. We're off.' So we all bolted from the field. I was running flat out with my head down, just hoping nothing would hit me. Bottles were being pelted from all directions. We all got off safely, but a flying bottle was only a couple of centimetres away from taking Tugga's head off.

We locked ourselves in the dressing room, and watched the crowd carrying on all over the ground. It was a shit-fight. It was really loud, and there was madness in their eyes. There was no way any player was going to go back onto the field with that sort of anger everywhere.

Tugga asked us what we wanted to do. I said there was no way I was going to field on the fence because all it would take was one bottle in the back of the head and that could be the end of me. Tom Moody wasn't keen either.

We were prepared for the game to be called off, but then the Barbados Police Commissioner came in and told us if we didn't go back out and play, our safety couldn't be guaranteed. I couldn't believe it. Security unable to guarantee safety! What sort of position did that put us in? So, Tugga asked us again what we wanted to do, and it was suggested that we re-call Sherwin. There had been a bit of debate before that, and it was our last option, but we didn't think we had any choice.

It was like a circus outside the dressing room. Sir Garfield Sobers went out to try to calm the crowd. He was a local legend, and if he couldn't do it how well were we going to go? Then it was announced Sherwin would be called back. The winning target and number of overs were reduced to make up for lost time, and by doing that the West Indies were virtually handed the game.

The ground was cleared of the crowd and we finally went back out, but there was still a lot of uncertainty in the team. I think most of us were still looking out of the corners of our eyes and over our shoulders.

The West Indies ended up winning, Sherwin made top score with 62. I was pretty pissed off when we walked from the field, but there was also a lot of relief. There were times during the incident when I was wondering how any of us were going to get out. It was the scariest moment I've ever had on a cricket field; I was really worried for my own safety, and all of my team-mates.

In the hotel afterwards I saw the run-out on TV. When we first dismissed Sherwin I thought it was his fault, but looking at the replay made me change my mind. I didn't realise BJ had his arms out so wide when the collision happened. It certainly would have made things hard for Sherwin. So in hindsight, calling him back was the right decision, even though we lost the game.

After the match, all the drama seemed a long way off when we stayed in Barbados for a week's holiday before the World Cup. It was sensational.

All the locals were really friendly, and no-one held anything against us. But nothing could excuse what had happened a couple of days earlier.

The holiday was exactly what we needed before heading to England. Tugga spoke about what was ahead, and how important it was for all of us to pull together as a team. He told us about his experiences the last time Australia won the World Cup in India in 1987. He said that team was successful because the players were hungry for success and wanted to win for each other. There was a real spirit and lots of self-belief. Basically he said if we were going to win in England we had to respect ourselves and each other. We also had to stick to our game plans and do the little things just as well as all the big things. He also stressed that our recent successes meant little when compared with what was ahead. We would be judged by what we did in the World Cup. The preparation had begun three years earlier when selectors started splitting the Test and limited-overs teams. Now it was up to us to prove that the right decisions had been made.

For me personally, the World Cup was a real mixture of highs and lows. I was picked ahead of Tom Moody for our first match against Scotland at Worcester, and although we won we didn't play well. Scotland made 7–181, and we got the runs four wickets down with five overs remaining. I didn't have to bat, and took 1–25 with the ball. It wasn't a great performance, but the whole team seemed a bit flat. We probably underestimated Scotland, and expected things to just happen in our favour. But the Scots played really well and made us work really hard, especially in the field. It was a disappointing start.

The next match against New Zealand in Cardiff was even worse. In the team meeting before the match we spoke about how the Kiwis were always a difficult side for us to play. We had to play well to beat them. But we didn't, and they won by five wickets. It was a disastrous game for me. I was run out for 2, took 0–24 off 6 overs, and hurt my knee while diving for a catch.

I was ruled out for the next game against Pakistan, and that gave Tom Moody the break. I didn't play another game on tour. It was much harder to take this time round than at the '96 World Cup because I'd been part of all the build-up at home and in the West Indies. I was really looking forward to it. I knew we were going to go well, and I thought this was my big chance to stamp my name on the international scene as a top-class all-rounder. It was the biggest personal disappointment of my career. But full credit to Tom. He came in and played a great role.

The whole tournament was a big challenge for us. We lost our third game against Pakistan, which meant we basically had to win every game from then on if we were going to be the champions. It was a huge ask, but Tugga never lost faith or confidence. He kept telling everyone to believe in their ability, and if they did that the team would be very hard to beat.

It turned out to be an amazing run home for us. The games against South Africa were unbelievable. The first one in the Super Six round at Headingley belonged to Tugga. He came in when we were 3–48 chasing 272 to win. I remember telling Damien Martyn that we would be going home the next day, but all of a sudden we were back in it. Tugga stayed in the middle all the way to the finish. His 120 not out was a brilliant innings. It would be hard to find an athlete in any sport who thrives on challenges as much as Tugga. People say he shows few emotions, but he can be as pumped as anyone. When he came back into the dressing room after that innings, he was really fired up. He was letting everyone know that we were going to win the World Cup. He sat down and said, 'Come on boys. We're going all the way here.' The win gave everyone a huge lift because we'd been bagged a bit in the media in previous matches, and some journalists had written us off. Tugga's innings showed everyone that the Australian team was back in a big way.

It was almost impossible to believe, but the semi-final against South Africa was an even better match. A tie. It was a huge game. When Damien Fleming started the last over, South Africa needed nine runs to win and we needed one wicket. Lance Klusener, who hits the ball as hard as any batsman I've ever seen, smashed the first two balls of Flem's over for four. It was all tied, and I thought to myself, 'Geez it's all over. This time we're definitely on our way home.' The next ball Klusener hit to Darren Lehmann at mid-on, Allan Donald had backed up too far at the bowler's end, and all Boof needed to do was hit the stumps, but he missed. The tension was incredible. And the rest is history. Klusener hit the next ball to

Mark Waugh at mid-off. Junior [Mark Waugh] flicked the ball to Flem, who underarmed it along the pitch to Gilly, who took the bails off. By this time Klusener and Donald were both at Flem's end after a huge mix-up. It was over. The match was a tie but we advanced to the final, having beaten the South Africans the game before. The dressing room soon turned into one big party. Everyone was shouting, hugging, and jumping around like schoolkids. I don't think anyone could really believe what had happened. The South Africans were shattered, but we didn't care. We were into the final, and that was all that mattered.

The final was an anti-climax. We beat Pakistan easily by eight wickets, and not surprisingly we partied really hard. One of the things that stands out about the celebrations was Tugga's consideration for the three players who weren't in the final. It was pretty well straight after we'd won, and Tugga was being swamped by well-wishers and the media, but he made a point of coming up to Brendon Julian, Damien Martyn and me. He told us that we were as much a part of the team as any other player, and he was very proud of our contributions. He said, 'Make sure you hold the trophy up when we get it. We all did this together.' It was really good of him to say that. It was a fantastic gesture. He's always thinking outside the obvious. It would have been easy for him to have been swept away by the moment, but he thought of his team-mates first. He was brilliant. I really admired him for that.

The highlight of the whole trip came hours after we'd won. Ricky Ponting was in charge of the team song, 'Underneath the Southern Cross', and he hadn't told anyone how he was going to do it. A few of us were beginning to wonder when it would happen, then all of a sudden Punter said, 'Boys, it's time. Follow me.' He then led us down from the dressing room, through the Lord's Long Room, and onto the field. We walked all the way out to the middle, then Punter got up on Tom Moody's shoulders and began the song. It was great. I had goosebumps. Nearly everyone else at the ground had gone home, so we had the home of cricket to ourselves. Gilly pretended to keep wicket. He put out beer cans where the ball had pitched for Warney's three wickets. Warney pretended to bowl, and the rest of us just yelled and appealed, and let ourselves go. It was probably not the most respectful thing we'd ever done, but we all enjoyed it. When we finally left the ground in the dark, the fun had only begun because the party back at the hotel went all night. There were some really sore heads and heaps of sunglasses worn the next day!

Overall, it was a bittersweet tour for me, but I'll never forget it. Being on the fringe made me more hungry for the next World Cup. It was a great lesson for me.

CHAPTER ELEVEN

AS GOOD AS IT GETS

Brett was a new person when he got rid of the back brace.
It was so good to see him excited and very keen to play
cricket again. We always knew he'd get there, but it was
tough for him.

Helen Lee

1998–99: another season, and another comeback for Brett. But unlike his first recovery from back problems, this time he was much more confident that he was well prepared for the rigours of fast bowling. His action had undergone significant modification: he was now a completely front-on bowler, beginning with a run-up that followed a straight line from the top of the bowling mark all the way through until the ball was delivered. He had also improved his front arm at the point of delivery, enabling it to act as a strong lever that pulled his body's momentum through the crease. Brett remembers how invaluable the endless hours in front of the mirror during winter had been:

In my early grade games for Mosman, I could still picture the images from the mirror in the back of my mind. I concentrated hard on everything that

I'd learnt. At first I was only bowling off about eight steps, but I slowly got more confident and kept going back a few more steps until I was back to my long run. By Christmas I was starting to bowl pretty quickly, and by the New Year I was back to full pace. It was a real thrill to be charging in again. At the start of the season I was a bit worried about what would happen with my back, but once I'd managed a few games I didn't think about it at all.

It seemed the injury worries had also drifted from the minds of NSW selectors, who chose Brett for the Sheffield Shield game against Victoria at the SCG the week before Christmas. Brett opened the bowling with Simon Cook, but both pacemen found the going tough in the drawn match in which the Bushrangers batted for 145 overs in their only innings of 9 declared for 438. Brett took 1–81 off 25 overs. It wasn't a remarkable return, but it was easy for fans and players alike to lose sight of the fact that it came in just Brett's fourth first-class outing.

Selectors showed faith in their 21-year-old quick by picking him for the Blues' four remaining Shield matches that season. It wasn't until the last game that Brett provided the return that his potential had long promised. He took 5–53 in the second innings against Tasmania on Hobart's notoriously flat Bellerive Oval pitch. It was his opening five-wicket haul in first-class cricket. NSW managed only first innings points in the drawn match, but Brett's match return of 7–124 had nevertheless left a lasting impression.

Team-mate Corey Richards recalls:

It was the quickest I'd seen him bowl since he'd come back from injury. It's hard to make batsmen rush their shots at Bellerive, but Brett was hurrying everyone. He had them jumping around, and in the second innings he was getting a lot of reverse swing. I was in the field thinking to myself, 'This bloke's gonna go all the way. There's no question about it.'

We went to Zimbabwe straight after that match on a special Academy tour, and Brett probably shouldn't have gone. He was just far too quick for those poor guys. He was breaking stumps and the batsmen were backing away. Brett just basically destroyed them. When he knew they were worried, he just bowled quicker. He took a heap of wickets and hit just as many guys in the head!

Among Helen Lee's collection of shoeboxes and memories is a folder full of faxed score sheets that show how destructive Brett was on the tour to Zimbabwe. In two one-day games against Matabeleland and Zimbabwe's Academy, Brett returned the respective match figures of 9 for 39 off 17.4 overs, and 8 for 52 off 19 overs. He returned home in early April 1999, not knowing just how close he was to making a much bigger international impact.

★ ★ ★

Even for the make-believe world of Hollywood, a visit by a group of international sportsmen to play cricket — a game which was as unfamiliar to Americans as lamingtons or Anzac Day — was most unusual. However, in September 1999 Tinseltown opened its arms and eyes to a series of cricket matches between an Australia 'A' team and the Indian 'A's. Although the results of the matches were of little importance, the tour was significant for Brett and Shane because it was the first time they'd gone on an overseas campaign together. It was the sign of things to come.

Brett remembers:

We were driving down Sunset Boulevarde in the team minibus. I looked across and saw the car behind us, and couldn't believe it. I knew the face, but for a moment it didn't click. Then all of a sudden I realised who it was and yelled, 'Have a look boys. That's Helen Hunt.' Her friend was driving. Helen had jeans on, no shoes, one foot halfway up the window, sunglasses, sunroof down. She drove past in this black car, so we started bipping the horn and waving.

After his brief brush with actress Helen Hunt, Brett returned to Australia full of hope for the 1999–2000 season, unaware of just how dramatically his career would take off — to steal a line from one of Hunt's movies, the approaching summer was to be 'As Good as it Gets'.

It began with Mosman. In just 53 overs in early season matches Brett took 12 wickets, a strike rate that prompted the NSW chairman of selectors, Alan Campbell, to suggest Sydney's grade ranks hadn't seen faster bowling since Jeff Thomson tormented batsmen 25 years earlier.

The impressive strike rate flowed into State matches. Brett took 2–43, 2–28, and 2–40 in the opening Mercantile Mutual Cup encounters, and he collected 12 scalps at 29.5 in the first three Pura Milk Cup games. His best return was 3–59 off 18.5 overs against South Australia in a rain-interrupted draw at the SCG. Steve Waugh was among his biggest supporters, and it wasn't a surprise to many critics that Brett, who'd turned 23 just a fortnight earlier, was included in Australia's squad for the Third, and final, Test of the series against Pakistan at the WACA ground in late November. He had played just 13 first-class matches.

Brett recalls:

It was a shock to be selected. I was sitting at home with Corey Richards watching Gilly [Adam Gilchrist] and Justin Langer smashing Pakistan in the Second Test in Hobart. Corey kept telling me he thought I was a chance of being picked for the next match, but I kept saying, 'No mate, no chance at all.' I wasn't thinking about it too much.

But about half an hour after the Hobart Test had finished, I got a phone call from Richard Watson of the ACB. He asked me what my plans were for the afternoon. I told him I wasn't doing anything special, then he replied, 'Well you better get some good clothes on. You'll be doing a presser [press conference] over at the NSW Cricket Association offices soon because you've just been chosen to go to Perth for the next Test.'

I almost dropped my drink, and I honestly felt like crying because it was a dream come true. I had to ask Richard to repeat what he'd said. I just couldn't believe it.

I was still on the phone when Corey began asking me what was going on. When he found out, he went straight to the fridge, got two beers, and was trying to throw one down my throat while I was still trying to take everything in from Richard on the other end of the phone. I was over the moon. It was about half past one; Richard was telling me all the things that had to be done, but all I wanted to do was call my parents. I rang them at about a quarter to two. Mum was at home, but Dad was at work, so I had to make a couple of calls to get on to him. Both were ecstatic. I then called Shane, Grant, my cousin Luke, and my best mate, Adam. All of them were really pumped and happy for me.

I was floating on a cloud. Twelve years of work had paid off. It was a huge honour; I felt as though I'd graduated from my apprenticeship. There was no relief, but just a really happy feeling. I had this flashback of all the problems I'd had with my back, and realised all the pain had been worth it.

Next, I rang my boss, Richard Bowman, at Barclays. He immediately arranged for me to come in and pick up a brand new suit. He was really excited, and wanted me to look good at the press conference.

Then it was off to the NSW offices for the announcement. It all went really quickly. The cameras, the questions, the flashes. I felt like I was in the middle of a dream.

By the time I got to Perth, there was a lot of hype about whether I'd be playing. It was going to come down to either me or Michael Kasprowicz. I didn't expect to play because Kasper was a great bowler with heaps of experience. I'd be lying if I said it wasn't hard to accept at first. I remember one net-session when the both of us were bowling flat chat, trying to impress as much as possible. Glenn McGrath and Damien Fleming both slowed down and tapered off, so there was only Kasper and me going flat out ball for ball against Justin Langer.

At the end of the session Steve Waugh came up to me and said, 'Sorry Brett, Kasper's been chosen, but it was a very close thing. Don't feel down about it. Just hang in there, just wait, you'll get your chance.' I was a little disappointed, but then I thought, 'Well at least I'm in the twelve, which means it's a good chance to experience everything that happens.' I saw it as a positive thing, and looking back I reckon it was the best thing that could have happened to me because I had the chance to get the feel of a Test match, the team, and the dressing room without the pressure of having to perform.

Being in the dressing room on the first day of the Test was a real buzz. I felt like a schoolboy who'd won a gold ticket prize. I'd always wondered what went on in the Australian room, and what went through the players' minds. I thought it would be pretty similar to what happened in the NSW room, but of a higher standard.

About 20 minutes before the start of play I was sitting quietly by myself when I looked over and saw Justin Langer brushing his Baggy Green cap. All I could think was how badly I wanted one. Then Steve Waugh got his cap out and rested it on his kit. I walked past to get a drink, looked at the inside of the cap, and saw dried blood from where he and Jason Gillespie had that collision in Sri Lanka a few months earlier. It gave me goosebumps. There was so much character in that cap. So much Steve Waugh.

Tugga [Steve Waugh] lost the toss and Pakistan were batting. Just before everyone went out onto the field, Tugga said, 'Come on boys, let's enjoy it firstly, let's play well, and do all the things we've spoken about.'

Ricky Ponting was really enthusiastic. He was firing the blokes up, saying, 'Come on guys, let's get out there and take them down. We're bloody better than them.' I kept thinking, 'Shit, how good is this?' I was really pumped, and I wasn't even playing! I went up and wished Kasper the best. I was really hoping he'd do very well because it was his life as well, and you can't wish any bad luck on a person. I just knew if I wanted to grab a spot I'd have to do better.

As the guys walked out the door, Pidgey [Glenn McGrath] and Flem got heaps of pats on the back. It was a great feeling to be part of it all.

The first time I had to run a couple of drinks around to Pidgey and Flem, I was really worried about what the crowd would say. Flem was bowling from the Lillee–Marsh Stand end, which meant I had to walk right round the fence. I was walking with my head bowed, floppy hat on, trying not to bring any attention to myself, but then some guys in the crowd started shouting, 'Lee, Lee.' So I waved, and that made them cheer. I really enjoyed it. I stood and signed a few autographs and was amazed how many people knew who I was. It really surprised me.

As I was walking back, a tennis ball landed 15 metres inside the field. It was in a break between overs, and I thought that I had two options: I could walk past, pretend not to see the ball, and get sledged; or I could duck onto the field, pick up the ball and fling it back into the crowd. I took the second choice, and the crowd cheered. I was really nervous, but the fans made me feel at home.

I was even more nervous the first time I ran a pair of gloves out. All I could think was, 'Don't trip over and look like a goose.' There was another time when I ran the wrong pair of gloves out for Punter [Ricky Ponting]. He has six or seven pairs of gloves, and he numbers them all. When he signalled for a pair I thought, 'Shit what pair does he want? I don't want to stuff up.' I chose his number threes, but when I got to the middle Punter said he wanted his fours. He was really good about it. He just told me to bring them out at the end of the next over. For the next six balls I was hoping that Punter wouldn't get out, otherwise he'd blame me. It's funny the things that ran through my mind. I was just like a work-experience kid.

The best part of the whole experience came after we'd won by an innings and 20 runs in only three days. We were in the dressing room, and some of the guys asked me if I knew the team song. I said I knew every word, and when the song began beer was being poured all over me, and the guys were saying congratulations on being part of the team. Singing the song was a very special moment. And being considered part of the team was even more special.

After a 3–0 clean sweep of the series against Pakistan, Australia turned its attention to a similar campaign against India. Still riding a wave of emotion, Brett was given the perfect platform to stake a position in the Test XI when NSW played the visitors at the SCG five days after the Perth Test. And he didn't disappoint: his display of fast bowling startled the Indians, and later prompted coach Kapil Dev to raise concerns about the legitimacy of Brett's action. Brett took 3–56 and 4–77, including a fiery spell late on the third day when he claimed two wickets in three balls. The delivery that bowled Test batsman VVS Laxman was reason enough to suggest Brett could trouble any top-class batsman with his pace alone.

India won the match, but the players were left wondering what would happen if they again met the quickest bowler they'd faced on tour. They didn't have to wait long for an answer because two days later Brett took 4–25 against them while playing for the Prime Minister's XI at Canberra's Manuka Oval. He claimed three scalps in his opening spell, including Sachin Tendulkar. The performance came on the heels of news that Brett had made way for medium-pacer and off-spinner Colin Miller for the First Test against India at the Adelaide Oval. It was a 'horses for courses' selection.

While the Australians launched their second series of the summer with a 285-run victory, Brett returned to the NSW team to take four wickets for the match in a heavy loss to Tasmania at the SCG. His second innings figures enhanced his chances of selection for the Second Test: 3–20 off 18 overs. His control was matched by his speed. In a near-deserted ground, the deliveries that smacked into the gloves of wicket-keeper Brad Haddin could be heard hundreds of metres away in the stands.

The Second Test against India was the traditional Boxing Day encounter at the Melbourne Cricket Ground. Brett had just one more Pura Milk Cup game to help push his causes. And his hopes were boosted by the game being played against Western Australia at the renowned haven for pacemen — the fast and bouncy WACA pitch in Perth. Brett says:

I was determined not to think too much about the Test team. But I must admit it was hard to keep out of my mind. There was a lot of talk in the papers about my chances, so I knew I was close to a call-up. But all I wanted to concentrate on was bowling well against Western Australia. NSW had most of its Test players back, and it was a good chance to impress them, as well as play with them and learn. It's not often a young player gets the chance to have the input of people like Steve Waugh. Tugga won the toss, and we batted first but struggled all the way to make 182.

When it came time to bowl, Tugga was really aggressive. He told me, 'Don't give half-volleys to these blokes because they're gonna try to pin you when you come in to bat, so get in there while you can.' He gave me a lot of confidence, and I just wanted to repay his faith in me.

I was pretty happy with my 4–84 in the first innings. I was bowling pretty quickly, but couldn't stop WA from making 312. Tugga and Michael Bevan both scored centuries in the second innings to set the Warriors 280 to win. When I began bowling in that second innings, I thought everything seemed in my favour. I had a bit of a breeze behind me, there were no footholes to worry me and I felt great. Luckily it was just one of those days when everything clicked. It was the quickest I think I've ever bowled, heaps quicker than against South Africa the following year when I clocked 156 kilometres an hour.

Mark Waugh told Shane in the slips that it was the fastest bowling he'd ever seen. At first I didn't realise how fast I was bowling. But there were a couple of balls that made me think that I was in a pretty good rhythm. I hit Ryan Campbell in the head with a bouncer, and later I bowled one to Jo Angel that took off well over his head. Brad Haddin went up, but the ball kept on sailing up and went one bounce into the sightscreen.

Most of the time fast bowling is about line and length, but there are times when you have to put the wind up a couple of batsmen. Dennis Lillee used to do it, so did Thommo, Geoff Lawson, and Merv Hughes. They all did it. It's a matter of mind games. You unsettle the batsman, then you get him out. I'm never out to hurt anyone but I do want to intimidate, and unfortunately Jo was the victim in that game. One ball kicked up about chest high to Jo, and a moment later I heard this huge crack when the ball hit his arm. Although Jo had a guard on, there was no protection *around his wrist. He hit the deck and his arm was shaking. He had to retire hurt with a broken wrist. I felt bad when it happened, but I knew I just had to turn around and get back to my mark to be ready for the next ball.*

I took 4–55, Stuart MacGill also claimed four wickets, and we won by 115 runs. Many of the guys came up to me afterwards and told me they'd never seen anything quicker. I only wish I'd had a speed gun there.

One of the best places to judge Brett's speed on that day was behind the stumps with the ball slapping into the gloves. NSW wicket-keeper Brad Haddin was in no doubt he'd never seen or felt a quicker or more lethal spell.

My first memory of the whole game was in Brett's very first over. I went back to where I normally stand to Brett, and decided to take a few extra paces back. Greg Hayne and Mark Waugh were next to me in the slips, and Mark Waugh said to us, 'What are you blokes doing standing this far back? I've never stood this far back for anyone.' Hayney and I told him we weren't going to move any closer. Then Brett came in and bowled his first ball, and Mark immediately said, 'Yep, you're right.' And he took a couple of steps back.

But the spell that everyone talks about came in the second innings. On that day I'd never seen batsman so scared to come to the wicket. I can remember Brad Williams and Sean Cary having a mid-wicket conference. Stuart MacGill was bowling from the other end with Brett at the time, and Cary and Williams agreed it was better to get out to MacGill than have to face Brett.

I've never seen a spell like it. The one ball that stands out is the bouncer that went sailing over my head and we all turned around in the slips to see if the ball would clear the boundary on the full. It half-volleyed into the fence, and was only half a foot from going all the way. Hayney and I looked at each other and said, 'Oh my God!' We actually felt scared for the batsmen. We felt it was unsafe for them. The slips cordon was standing way back past the 30-metre circle and we had a lot of time to see the ball, but I would have hated being one of the batsmen. It was hard enough keeping. I had to be on the ball, otherwise I would have been in a lot of trouble. I never saw Jeff Thomson bowl or any of the really quick bowlers from that era, but I can't imagine them being any quicker than Brett on that day.

Brett's display left lasting impressions. Test batsman Justin Langer had played a rocket onto his stumps, and Adam Gilchrist was beaten for pace when he attempted a pull shot that went skywards and offered Brett a simple return catch. It was rumoured that one Warriors player told a team-mate that if he was to attempt a hook shot, he'd better start swinging before Brett let go of the ball. In his post-match interviews, Steve Waugh was adamant that Brett was quicker than Pakistan's spearhead Shoaib Akhtar.

It wasn't surprising that Brett stole the headlines, and there were even less raised eyebrows when the Boxing Day Test team was announced. Brett remembers:

I was pleased to get another chance so quickly after the Perth Test. At least this time I knew a little bit about what to expect, but I was still really apprehensive and didn't want to interfere with anyone else's preparation. One of my first memories of the whole experience began on Christmas Eve. It was my first one away from home. Mum and Dad weren't coming down, and Shane wasn't going to be in Melbourne until the Test started. I sat in my room, but didn't want to ring any of the team to see what they were up to because I knew everyone had family and friends and would be doing their own thing. The last thing I wanted anyone to think was, 'Geez this Brett guy is a bit of nuisance.' So, I thought I'd go for a walk by myself and maybe buy a CD. I ended up running into Gilly and his wife Mel. They asked if I had any family with me, and when I said no they told me I had to make sure I got involved with all the team's family activities on Christmas Day.

The following morning I woke up and saw a gift under my door. It was an Eric Clapton CD with a card on it from Gilly and Mel. Apart from the obvious Christmas tidings, Gilly wrote that he hoped we played heaps of Test cricket together. I thought it was one of the nicest gestures ever.

Christmas morning was spent with the team and their families and then in the afternoon we had training and a team meeting. I had a great day. But that night I really started thinking about the game. Was I going to play or was I going to be twelfth man behind Kasper again? I rang home, and also called my best mate, Adam, just to put my mind at ease. I went through the same sort of routine that I normally did before a match. I had a bit of pasta and just wanted to relax, but thoughts started creeping in: Should I start changing things now that I might be playing for Australia? Was it going to be different if I played in the Test? I had to tell myself, 'Don't be stupid. Just keep doing the same things that have got you here.'

On Boxing Day morning, we had a light training run. Shane Warne walked past me and said, 'If you play today Binga, good luck mate. Just go out there and get them. Go out there and lap it up.' Warney had taken me under his wing in many ways, and had told me the most important thing was to back myself and have fun. He said Test cricket was just like playing first grade with very, very good first graders. It was like playing Shield cricket with very, very good Shield players. He tried to simplify it and stressed that Test cricket was still just a game, and if I kept doing the things I had been doing I would succeed. He recalled his first Test when he was torn apart by Ravi Shastri at the SCG. He said it was a great lesson because he never lost faith in his own ability. It was a very good piece of advice. Warney was fantastic. He made me really relaxed.

At the end of training, we got into a group. John Buchanan said a few things, then it was over to Tugga to announce the team. Before I knew it, Kasper was congratulating me and wishing me luck. I was in!

The presentation of the Baggy Green happened out on the ground before play began. To be honest, I can't remember who gave me the cap because I was in my own world. The team stood around, but all I could see was this Baggy Green in a man's hands. There was a little speech and, although I was listening, nearly all my attention was on the cap. I just wanted to get it. 'Give it to me please. Give it to me.' Then the man reached for my hands, shaking one and putting the cap in the other. I felt my heart racing. All I could do was look down at the cap and feel it in my hands. Then Pidgey tapped me on the shoulder and said: 'Great stuff, Binga.' All the guys came up and wished me luck. When I saw Tugga, I asked if I could put the cap on. He nodded: 'Put it on, mate. You've earnt it.'

So I put it on and the crowd cheered, which gave me goosebumps. Dennis Lillee had told me earlier that my debut Test would be the greatest moment of my life. It was a moment I'll hold on to forever.

I was so keen to get out on the field and get going, but rain meant only a couple of hours were possible on the first day. We batted, so I had no role to play. That night I didn't want to leave the Baggy Green in the dressing room, so I took it home with me. All I wanted to do was sleep with it on my head, but then I thought, 'No you idiot, you'll crush it, and you can't do that!' So I put it beside my bed. The next morning, it was the first thing that I put in my bag. Unfortunately the rain came again, so I spent another restless day inside watching our batsman do the work.

The rest of the Test was just a dream. After making 27 on the third morning, I was really pumped up to bowl well. The guys were right behind me from the start. Pidgey really tried to look after me as his new ball partner. He told me not to worry about trying to outdo any other bowler, because the day I started to do that would be the day I failed. His advice was simple: 'Just worry about what you have to do, and the rest will look after itself.' Since then I've learnt so much from Glenn. I admire him because of his patience and his line. He's the king of bowling in the corridor.

I have a lot of memories from that first Test. Obviously standing at the top of my mark to bowl my first ball was a really special time. Because of the weather interruptions, that didn't happen until just before lunch on the third day. The crowd gave me a huge cheer, and that gave me a lot of confidence. I felt as though I was dreaming four balls later when I cleaned up Sadagopan Ramesh for my first Test wicket. That alone would have made me happy, but I was lucky enough to also get Rahul Dravid in my second spell. It was a bad ball and a bad shot, Dravid flashed at a wide one outside off-stump, and Gilly took an easy catch. I couldn't believe that I'd got a wicket in Test cricket with such an ordinary delivery, but I knew there'd be other days when no matter how well I bowled I'd come up empty-handed. So, it was a case of enjoying the good times while they lasted. It's surprising how quickly everything happened that day. Especially my fourteenth over. It was the fifth over of my third spell, and I was still running on adrenalin. It was late in the day and the ball was reverse swinging, which is a great weapon for a fast bowler to have against the lower order. You can nearly always back yourself to get three of the tail by bowling Irish. I went for a yorker with my first ball, but it ended up being a shin-high full toss that swung in late and bowled Manavva Prasad. Luck was on my side. The next ball I went for another yorker and this time I got it right. Ajit Agarkar played too late and was hit on the boot. I don't think I've ever appealed louder in my career. Gilly and the whole slips cordon went up with me, and umpire David Shepherd put his finger up. I was on a hat-trick in my first Test. All the guys were pumping me up, and we were laughing in the huddle. Then when I went back to my mark, Tugga ran up from gully to have a quick chat. Believe it or not, I can't remember what he said because I was just too excited. I had a good think about what I would bowl, and since the ball was swinging Irish so well I decided to keep it full again, aim wide of off-stump and hope that it came in late. The atmosphere was incredible. Fans were banging the boundary fence as I ran in to bowl, and the noise just echoed around the ground. Unfortunately I overcompensated for the swing and pitched the ball too wide and Javagal Srinath pushed it to cover. I wasn't disappointed. How could I be? I'd already taken four wickets, and with the last ball of the over Srinath gloved a short one to Mark Waugh at second slip. Three wickets in an over, and five on debut. It had to be a fairy tale.

Although we were on top we couldn't stop Sachin Tendulkar from getting 116. The difference in class between himself and every other Indian batsman was amazing. His ability to whip the ball from outside off-stump to the leg-side made him really hard to bowl to. But the most obvious thing about his batting was the amount of time he had to play every shot. He never seemed in a hurry, which was amazing considering he had such a heavy bat, which he still managed to wave around like a toothpick. It was a good lesson bowling to him because I learnt just how little room for error there is against the top Test batsmen. He scored 52 in the second innings, and looked on his way again until Warney trapped him lbw. I was lucky enough to get two wickets in that innings, but more importantly we won by 180 runs, and stretched Australia's unbeaten Test run to six matches. At the end the guys were running to grab the stumps, and although I wanted one I didn't want to look greedy in my first game, so I stood back. As we were walking off, Pidgey had his arm around me and was saying, 'Well bowled Binga. This is Test cricket. It's great fun, isn't it?' Just as he finished saying it, Justin Langer tapped me on the shoulder and said, 'Congratulations, "five-for" in your first Test. Well played.' Then he gave me a stump. He didn't have to do that, but it made me feel very much a part of the side.

There was one downside to the Test: In my final few overs of the third day I started feeling pain from injuries that I'd put up with for a couple of seasons. Posterior ankle impingements, two bones rubbing at the back of the ankles, sent pain shooting up my Achilles tendons. It felt like I was running on steak knives. In previous seasons I'd gone through so much tape to support the injuries, but the pain was getting worse and worse. I'd been OK at the beginning of the season, but when I started landing in footholes later on in my spells I felt a lot of pain. So I tried going out wider and wider to avoid the holes. There were times when the commentators praised me for using the crease so well, but little did they know I was doing it because it hurt so much.

For the first 15 overs of the Boxing Day Test I didn't feel a thing, but the last four overs were really painful, almost unbearable. The first ball of each new over I'd almost have a tear in my eye, but being a fast bowler I thought I had to put up with these sorts of things. There had been days when I'd come off the field, pulled my shoes off, and found my socks full of blood and a busted toenail or two. Dennis Lillee had helped me deal with pain. He said I could expect all sorts of problems, from sore toenails to shins, back, shoulders, but he said I could prove how good I was if I could bowl through them. So that was the way I looked at the impingements. They were just some of the joys of being a fast bowler.

I put up with the pain again for the Third Test in Sydney. The match meant a lot to me: not only would I be playing on my home ground, but

Mum and Dad were going to be there to watch. There's nothing better than having your parents cheer you on, and I wanted to make them proud. And it seemed half of Wollongong came up to join them!

It was a very prestigious occasion because we had the honour of wearing the special skull caps to mark the new millennium. They were replicas of the caps worn in 1900. It was also Mark Waugh's 100th Test, which made us play that little bit harder.

Walking out there with the team made me think back to a year ago when I was in the stands watching. Back then, I imagined what it would be like playing in front of a big crowd on my home ground. Now I didn't have to imagine any more. As I went down the walkway and onto the field, members and fans were slapping me on the back wishing me luck. I thought to myself, 'It can't get any better than this. It just can't.'

But being on a hat-trick in the first innings made me think again! It was a spine-tingling few minutes. I got Vijay Bhardwaj caught behind, then Ajit Agarkar edged one to Mark Waugh for his fourth golden duck in a row! For the second Test running, Javagal Srinath came out to face the hat-trick ball. I couldn't help having a huge grin on my face when I was walking back to the top of my mark. I wasn't nervous. I thought I had a really good chance. I was going to bowl an inswinging yorker because the ball was starting to go Irish by that stage. As I turned to run in, a really fast hand clap started all round the ground. I must have run in heaps quicker than I should have. And like I did in Melbourne, I got a little bit too excited. But it was hard not to get carried away because the crowd's cheering was going right through me. Tugga said afterwards that it was the loudest roar he'd heard on a cricket ground. Unfortunately it didn't help me get the wicket though, but it didn't worry me. The most important thing was that Australia was doing well, and I was having fun. Above all else I was enjoying myself.

I ended up taking six wickets for the match, and we won by an innings and 141 runs again in only three days. We partied very hard that night. We sat in the dressing room for hours and hours. I remember sitting next to Pidgey for a long time as we just laughed and talked over a beer. At one stage I looked around the room and thought, 'Christ I'm here with all my *idols. Can you believe it, Binga?' For so many years I'd watched them on TV, read about them in magazines, and worshipped them. Then in the blink of an eye I was sitting next to them celebrating a Test series win. That was the first time I had to pinch myself to think that it was all really happening. If someone had told me a year earlier that I'd be in the Australian team by the end of the 2000 summer, I would have laughed at them. It is still hard to believe.*

It was a magnificent start to Brett's international career. In just two matches he had taken 13 wickets at 14.15, his pace and boyish enthusiasm adding another dimension to an already versatile attack. Wiping the spray of champagne from his eyes in the dressing room after the Test, he discovered he had more reasons to celebrate than those inspired by his performances and his team-mates' clean sweep of the Test summer. He had been picked in Australia's 13-man squad for the Carlton & United Series against India and Pakistan. And he wouldn't be the only Lee.

CHAPTER TWELVE

THE FAMILY REUNION

We are very, very proud of them. Only the parents really understand the effort it takes.

Bob Lee

Despite his World Cup inclusion, Shane was not an ACB contracted player for the 1999–2000 season. After missing selection for tours to Sri Lanka and Zimbabwe in September and October, he was once again having to prove his worth to selectors at the start of the home summer. His campaign began when he scored 19 and failed to take a wicket in the Blues' seven-wicket loss to Victoria at North Sydney Oval in a Mercantile Mutual Cup match. However, his fortunes and level of responsibility changed for the following Pura Milk Cup and Mercantile Mutual Cup encounters against Queensland at the Gabba. Regular captain Michael Bevan was in Zimbabwe, leaving Shane as stand-in skipper, a position he relished. He almost led the Blues to a dignified draw in the Pura Milk Cup match when he scored a valiant 98 in the second innings. He had earlier taken 4–87 off 26 overs in the Bulls' first innings. In the Mercantile Mutual Cup match, Shane's all-round performance shone brightly as NSW came back from the brink of embarrassment to beat the home side by four wickets. Choosing to bat after winning the toss, the Bulls were well placed to make a massive score after Matthew Hayden (104) and Jimmy Maher (87) blasted the bowlers in a 187-run opening stand off just 35 overs. However, Shane and Stuart MacGill led a fightback by taking three wickets each as Queensland's middle and lower order stumbled its way to 9 for 247.

Shane recalls:

That match was the perfect example of how quickly luck can change. We were in all sorts of trouble, and for a while I was thinking, 'Geez how do we get out of this?' But Stuart MacGill bowled really well, and Brett bowled with great control at the end to take two wickets and keep Queensland under 250. It was still a really big chase, but the pitch was a good batting strip, and I just had a feeling it could be a special day. I'd hit the ball really well in the Pura Milk game, and was pretty confident. But our batsmen started the way our bowlers had. We lost Slats, Rod Davison, and Corey Richards early, and were in trouble at 3–49. When Graeme Rummans came out to join me, I just told him to have some fun, play some shots and see what happened. I could see that he relaxed and gained some confidence because I didn't put any pressure on him. The next thing you know we'd added 70, and were on our way. We ended up putting on 180, and it was a real pity that Graeme got out for 67 when we were only a handful of runs short of winning. We got the runs with four wickets and four overs to spare. It was a great win, one of the most satisfying of my career because we'd been down and out twice in the match and could have easily just given in. But everyone fought really hard, and showed a lot of character. It was also satisfying because I'd scored my first domestic limited-overs century. I was most pleased because I'd performed with the bat under pressure, something that I'd not always done.

Shane scored 112 off just 97 deliveries. The innings included two towering sixes off one over from paceman Andy Bichel. The first six landed on the top tier of the Gabba grandstand, leaving Shane in no doubt it was the biggest hit of his career. His Man-of-the-

Match performance was the perfect platform from which to launch his campaign for an Australian recall.

Unlike previous seasons, his bowling was keeping pace with his batting. In his best start with the ball in a home summer, he took 11 wickets at 20.54 in the first three Pura Milk Cup matches. His good form continued in the limited-overs arena when he claimed 1–37 off 9 overs, and blasted 46 from just 36 balls in the Blues' 21-run victory over Tasmania at North Sydney Oval. He was rewarded for his early-season consistency when named captain of the Prime Minister's XI to play India in Canberra. Although Brett stole many of the headlines with his four-wicket haul, Shane further elbowed the national selectors after hammering 55 off 38 deliveries, and taking 2–27 in an impressive support role to his brother. The Prime Minister's XI won by 164 runs after making a record score of 5–344. Queensland's Andrew Symonds scored 101 off 90 balls, and versatile Victorian Ian Harvey played a lesser role, scoring 19 off 13 balls and taking two wickets. All three all-rounders were on the edge of Australian selection, and were given further chances to impress when they were picked in the 'A' squad to play two matches against Pakistan in Perth and Adelaide. Shane was again chosen to lead the side. Shane says:

Although we were all competing for spots in the Australian side, I tried not to think about it. There had been times earlier in my career when I was really aware of what other players did, and I kept thinking if I didn't outperform them on any day I'd fall behind when it came to selection time. But experience taught me just to look after what I had to do. Being worried about others is a trap that can affect many young, inexperienced players. You spend so much time looking over your shoulder that you can't concentrate properly on your own game. It can be a hard habit to break, and it really only comes with having confidence in your own ability. You always have to back yourself. It's yet another valuable thing I've learnt from Steve Waugh. No matter what the situation, he always gives the impression that he can come out on top. I wanted to take a similar attitude into the Australia 'A' matches. They were really important games for me, and I wanted to remain confident that I could handle any challenge that was thrown my way.

Brett's selection in the Test team gave me an added reason to perform. At the time the 'A' team was chosen, Brett was preparing for his second Test in Sydney. It had given me goosebumps when he'd first gone out onto the MCG for his debut Test. It was really exciting for me. And one of the first things I thought was, 'Now I've gotta pull my finger out if I want to join him and have some fun.' It inspired me to think that one day we could be playing for Australia together. If he did well in the Sydney Test there was no doubt he'd be in the one-day squad. It was now up to me to make sure I was there with him.

The prospects of a family reunion moved closer after Shane led the 'A's to two easy victories. They won by 52 runs at the WACA. Shane took 4–32 and scored 11 off 12 balls in a match dominated by an opening stand of 191 between Matthew Hayden (128) and David Fitzgerald (85). Two days later Shane scored an unbeaten 60 off 63 balls to guide his team to a six-wicket win at the Adelaide Oval. Earlier, medium-pacer Paul Wilson and leg-spinner Stuart MacGill had taken three wickets each in Pakistan's disappointing total of 167. Shane had failed to take a wicket, but his batting had ensured he was another step closer to joining his brother. By the end of the day, the family reunion was guaranteed when Australia announced its squad for the first four games of the Carlton & United Series. Shane remembers:

It was a great honour. We spoke to each other on the phone, and neither of us could wait to get together and get into it. There was a huge build-up before those one-dayers because there was a fair bit of excitement in the media about Australia having two sets of brothers in the one team. The first game was in Brisbane against Pakistan. Brett made his debut, but I missed out. It was hard watching Brett from the dressing room. We were so close to being together in the team that I found it one of the toughest games I've ever had to sit out. I wished him luck, and was probably more nervous than he *was when he went onto the field. Tugga kept him back until second change, and he didn't take a wicket in what was an ordinary start to our series. We were chasing only 185 to win, but were rolled for 139. Brett made only 2.*

I was really disappointed that I didn't play, but Tugga told me I'd get my chance in the second game against India in Melbourne. When the team was announced, it was a really proud moment. Brett and I would be out there together. I had to pinch myself and ask, 'Is this really happening?' In the dressing room before play Brett and I really encouraged each other. It didn't seem that long ago that we were in Mum and Dad's backyard pretending to play for Australia. Now we were actually doing it for real.

Australia won by 28 runs. Shane made an important contribution in the final overs when he hit 22 off just 15 balls. However, neither he nor his brother played significant roles at the bowling crease. Shane took 1–57 off 10 overs, and Brett, bowling first change behind Glenn McGrath and Damien Fleming, went wicket-less. The first two matches of his international limited-overs career were in sharp contrast to his Test fortunes.

The match was scarred by a crowd disruption in the latter stages after a mix-up on the electronic scoreboard. The third umpire was called upon to judge a run-out involving century-maker Saurav Ganguly. Initially a green light was shown on the scoreboard but it was quickly replaced by a red light, signalling Ganguly's departure and prompting hundreds of bottles to be hurled onto the field from a group of Indian supporters in the Great Southern Stand. It was Brett's first taste of unruly crowd behaviour, and the prelude to what would happen just a few months later in New Zealand.

Australia enjoyed a five-wicket victory in the next match against the Indians at the Sydney Cricket Ground. Brett again bowled first change, claiming his initial one-day victim when middle-order batsman Devang Ghandi offered Michael Bevan a catch at mid-wicket. Both Lees finished with a wicket each on a greentop that saw the visitors crumble for just 100.

Shane overshadowed his younger brother three days later in Melbourne when Australia cruised to a six-wicket win over Pakistan. The more experienced Lee took 3–24, while Brett claimed 1–37.

It was turning into a profitable series for Shane. He finished the preliminary matches with 11 wickets, including a best haul of 4–37 off 8.5 overs when Australia beat Pakistan by 15 runs in Melbourne. His batting was explosive. Before the finals he'd tallied 94 runs off just 69 deliveries, each of his five innings coming in the furious swirl of the closing overs.

Shane acknowledges:

It was a great series for me. Once I'd got back into the team, there was no way in the world I was going to let go. I'd done a bit of soul searching while I was on the outer, and it made me realise how hard I had to work if I was going to succeed. There were times in the past when I'd been tagged with an 'easy come-easy go' attitude, and although I didn't agree with it, perception is reality. It is everything. Justin Langer is like that. Everyone knows how hungry, tough and committed he is because he has worked really hard on it from day one. I wanted to show everyone that I was also 100 per cent committed to playing well, and my performances started to show that. I was particularly pleased with my bowling. Throughout my career I'd been inconsistent, but now I was getting on a bit of a roll and was looking forward to getting the ball in my hand in every match. It's a great feeling when you know you have contributed significantly to a team's performance, and I felt as though I was doing that. There was a sense of relief because I was starting to live up to my own expectations. I hadn't yet reached my potential, but I was getting there. I still believed I had a lot more to offer.

Brett followed Shane's lead. Despite a slow start to the series, he left few critics in any doubt that he was an extraordinary talent when he took 5–27 off 8.5 overs against India at the Adelaide Oval.

After losing its first game of the series Australia had gained considerable momentum, winning its remaining seven preliminary matches to enter as the hot favourite in the best-of-three finals series against Pakistan. The first match at the MCG was only the second time throughout the campaign that Brett opened the bowling. And it was the first occasion he'd shared the new ball with Glenn McGrath. What followed in the opening overs of Pakistan's innings was a relentless display of pace bowling. Pakistan slumped to 5–28 after McGrath had taken three wickets in seven balls. He finished with 3–17, while Brett took 3–18 in a meagre total of 154. Australia won by six wickets, and two days later wrapped up the series after a display that demoralised the visitors. Defending 7 for 337, the Australians watched McGrath again cut through the top order with clinical precision. Pakistan stumbled to 185, McGrath, the chief destroyer, taking 5–49, and Brett claiming 3–51.

It was the end of a memorable international summer for both Lees. They each finished the series with 16 wickets, just three behind McGrath, who not surprisingly was the most successful bowler. Shane was easily the most aggressive batsman in the competition, scoring 106 runs at an average of 26.5 and a formidable strike rate of 132.5.

But there was no time to bask in their efforts. A challenging, and at times frightening, trip across the Tasman was looming.

CHAPTER THIRTEEN

THREE STRIPES AND YOU'RE OUT

I suppose it does mean a lot to me to reach the 100-mile barrier, and one day everything might be so much in my favour that I will be able to have a real crack at the mark. But if it never happens, it won't worry me.

Brett Lee

Just a week after winning the Carlton & United Series, Australia's limited-overs players departed for six matches against New Zealand. Throughout the series there was little evidence to counter Kiwi captain Stephen Fleming's claim that the Australians were a stronger combination than the World Cup-winning squad. Australia won 4–1 after the first encounter in Wellington was abandoned when rain destroyed the match after just 23 overs.

In the second game at Auckland's Eden Park, Brett was named the Man of the Match after taking 3–21 off seven overs, signalling a warning to the home side for the rest of the campaign. He also took a remarkable catch that remains in the minds of everyone who saw it.

Brett remembers:

It was the flukiest snare I've ever taken. There was no skill involved in it at all. Glenn McGrath bowled a short one to Chris Cairns, who got a top edge. Because the ground was so short square of the wicket, I was quite square at fine-leg. When Chris hit the ball I thought it was going to bounce somewhere in front of the sightscreen. I had visions of running round, grabbing it, then flicking it back to Gilly. I began sprinting after it and was getting ready to do a diving save, but it kept carrying and carrying. All of a sudden I thought, 'I'm half a sniff here.' I was bolting, then the next thing you know I'd actually over-run the ball because it was swirling. So I stopped in a hurry, and threw my left hand out behind me. It was just one of those freakish things because the ball couldn't have gone into my hand any more perfectly. It just stuck beautifully. I couldn't believe it. I jumped up, looked at the boys and grinned. When we got together most of the guys said, 'You arsey bastard. How could you have taken that?' It will be a long time before I take another one like that again. That's if I ever do.

It was also a pleasing match for Shane, who claimed 2–27 in Australia's five-wicket win, but sadly he most remembers the match for its crowd disturbances:

New Zealand only made 122, and they were always up against it, so I suppose the crowd got a bit bored and frustrated because we were on top. Towards the end of the innings, spectators started throwing bottles and fruit at anyone fielding near the fence. Brett and Glenn McGrath copped most of it, but a few things came my way as well. It was nowhere near as bad as in the West Indies the previous year, but it still annoyed me. I know there is a rivalry. You can be passionate about supporting your team, but you don't have to go over the top. I don't see how people can get so uptight about a sport because it really is only a game. Some fans are just narrow-minded.

They can be funny people, New Zealanders. It's almost as if they have a big chip on the shoulder when it comes to comparisons against Australia. They think so personally. They build up a rivalry between us and them, but I don't think it's as fierce as the rivalry between us and England. You expect to cop a bit of stick when you're fielding on the fence in another country, that's all part and parcel of it. Normally it's a bit of a joke, and the players can smile or laugh it off. But it's a bit different when you're hearing: 'You're a f. . . ing c. . . t!' all day. And that's what was happening that day. It was disgraceful, and left a really sour taste. The New Zealand players are good blokes, but some of their fans need a real wake-up.

The disturbances proved just a dress rehearsal for what happened in the next contest — a day/nighter at Carisbrook, Dunedin. Brett recalls it was just one delivery that ensured he played a leading role:

We'd batted pretty well to make 4–310 on a good deck. We knew we'd have to work hard for the wickets, especially when Nathan Astle started hitting us around a bit. He ended up making 81, and Roger Twose kept up the chase with 62. Once he was out, Chris Harris and Adam Parore were the last two big hopes for New Zealand. Harris was batting really sensibly, and I knew Parore was the one I had to attack. I'd copped a bit of punishment earlier, so I was really keen to make up for it. After pitching a few up, I banged in a shorter one which climbed pretty quickly. It hit Adam's glove, then knocked his helmet off onto the stumps. It was an unfortunate way to get out, but it was a legitimate wicket. Adam started to walk off, he seemed quite happy to go, but then he turned around when he saw the umpires having a chat about whether the ball had gone above shoulder-height. Replays were being shown around the ground, and a lot of people started booing and jeering. Then the umpires confirmed that Adam was out, and that's when the crowd went absolutely berserk. They started to light things, and threw whatever they had onto the field. Cans, bottles, fruit, even pieces of wood. I thought, 'Geez this is just meant to be a game. What are they doing?' At the end of the over I went down to fine-leg, and blokes over the fence started abusing me. They said that I was rubbish, and they were going to kill me. I didn't mind the sledges because they are part of sport, but I couldn't cop things being thrown. There were cans everywhere on the ground, and I got hit on the back of the head with a plum. I turned around and saw only three security guards among thousands of people, and thought that there was no control over the crowd at all.

At this stage all the outfielders went back into the middle and told Tugga what was happening. He was pretty angry because he has always been outspoken about bad crowd behaviour. Play was stopped for about 10 minutes while the ground was cleared up. It was a new experience for me, and one that I would have been glad never to see again. I actually felt quite frightened.

We ended up winning the game by 50 runs to equal England's world-record run of being unbeaten in 12 consecutive one-dayers. But many of us will remember the game for all the wrong reasons.

Shane didn't play that game, but he too has unsavoury memories of it, and what happened afterwards:

Dunedin is a university town, and many of the crowd that day were students. They'd been drinking for much of the time, and some were really aggressive by the end. Our team manager, Steve Bernard, congratulated the team on a good win, but suggested no-one went out that night. He said we'd just have a few drinks back at the team hotel, and make it a quiet night.

On the way back to the hotel, Mark Waugh wanted a quick bite. So we stopped the team bus and went into a McDonald's. It was just closing up, but there were a heap of people in there from the cricket. Some started to give us a bit of stick, and one bloke in particular was giving Matthew Hayden a really hard time. Matt basically told him to pull his head in and leave him alone. But the guy started to get really abusive and personal. He was easy to recognise because he had this old Adidas shirt on.

We managed to get back on the bus without any further problems, but the next morning there was a knife in one of the tyres of the team bus. It had a note attached to it which threatened Matt and his family. It was addressed by 'Adidas Three Stripes'. We reported it to the police, and we had no more worries after that. But it did make me realise just how much we took for granted. It would be so easy for a high-profile player like Warney or Steve Waugh to be targeted by some psycho fan with an agenda. It's frightening to think what could happen. Hopefully it never will, but it is a possibility.

At least one player exacted some revenge in the fourth match at the tiny Jade Stadium ground in Christchurch. Adam Gilchrist had spectators ducking for cover as he plundered 128, including seven sixes, off only 98 deliveries in Australia's massive total of 6–349. Shane remained 4 not out, and both he and Brett later came in for some punishment when New Zealand's batsmen adopted an all-out approach to the run chase. Shane took 2–51 off 9 overs, and Brett suffered the worst figures of his brief limited-overs career when he was taken for 59 runs in 9 wicket-less overs. Australia won the match by 48 runs to extend their unbeaten streak to 13 games, a new world record. They won again in the fifth match at McLean Park, Napier, but New Zealand finally struck success when the teams returned to Eden Park for the last game. Shane and Brett played limited roles as the series wound down.

While the Australians turned their attention to three Tests against the Kiwis, Shane returned to the NSW team for its final Pura Milk Cup match of the season against Western Australia in Sydney. It was a disaster. Despite one full day being lost to rain, the Blues were thrashed by an innings and 34 runs. Shane made only 25 and 10, and took 0–49. It was an emotional letdown after playing such a leading role with Australia. The Blues had suffered their worst season in history, winning just one match and losing eight outright. They'd also failed to secure one first-innings victory. They finished a creditable third in the Mercantile Mutual Cup competition, but it was little consolation.

Because of their Australian duties, Shane and Brett missed about half of the NSW season. In six Pura Milk Cup matches, Shane's return was 267 runs at 22.25 and 17 wickets at 23.71. Brett took 24 wickets at 23.96 and scored 100 runs at 14.29 in only five games. With his international career blossoming, it seemed certain his future role for his State would be limited to even less appearances:

The New Zealand tour showed me how little State cricket the Test guys now play. If you ask every one of them, they would love the chance to devote more time and effort to their states, but it's just not possible. When you're a Test player, the best way to help your state is by making it proud of you when you wear the Baggy Green. Hopefully I achieved that against the Kiwis.

I have various memories of the three Tests in New Zealand. In the first match at Eden Park the personal highlight came in the final few overs of the opening day. We'd batted first after winning the toss, but were rolled for only 214 on an uneven pitch. When it was time to bowl, I actually came on second change because we opened with Colin Miller, and Warney bowled first change. It was starting to get a little dark and the ball was really moving about, so I knew I had a chance of getting a catch to the slips. And that's what happened. Craig Spearman nicked one to Damien Martyn, who took an absolute screamer in the gully. New Zealand were three wickets down at that stage, and they decided to send in Craig Wiseman as a nightwatchman. When it came to the last over, the strike was turned over to Wiseman with three balls to go. Tugga came up to me and said he was going to put in a bat pad. He said Wiseman would expect the short one so we'd give him one, then keep the next two right up to him. I bowled a bouncer, then a full one which Wiseman played and missed. So we had one ball left for the day. Tugga approached me again and asked what I was thinking. I told him it was going to be full and quick. So I steamed in, kept it full, Wiseman played too late, and the ball knocked his stumps out. I just went berserk and jumped in the air. It was one of the most memorable wickets I'd ever taken.

But it couldn't compare with when Warney got Wiseman in the second dig. Wiseman went to play a sweep, the ball brushed his glove, Gilly took the catch, and the whole team yelled. It was Warney's 356th wicket, beating Dennis Lillee's Australian record of 355. It was a great moment to be on the field. A few of us had actually had a bit of chat before the game about what we'd thought Warney would do when he broke the record. Would he throw a cartwheel? Go down on one knee and pump his fist? No-one was sure. But when it came to the real celebration, Warney was actually quite cool about it. He simply put his hand in the air. I think it was probably a huge relief for him because there'd been a lot of build-up in the media. It was great for him to pass that mark. I felt so happy and proud of him because he'd worked so hard to achieve it. We won by 62 runs and headed to Wellington for the Second Test.

I most remember the match at the Basin Reserve because I bowled what I thought was my best wicket-taking ball up to that stage of my career. It was when I knocked over Matthew Sinclair for a duck with an inswinger in the second innings. It was one of the quickest balls I bowled on tour, and was very similar to the delivery that cleaned up Ramnaresh Sarwan in the First Test against the West Indies later in the year. Glenn McGrath was kind enough to rate the Sarwan dismissal as the ball of the summer.

I copped a bit of punishment at the Basin against one of the best hitters in cricket. In the first innings, I was bowling pretty quickly when Chris Cairns came in, but it didn't worry him at all. He top-edged a bouncer for six, then the next over I bowled a pretty good length ball that he smashed straight back over my head into the stands. When I looked back at him he winked, as if to say, 'This is a real good Test here, mate. Let's see what you've got.' He really wanted to take me apart, and he did that day. He scored 109, and got 69 in the second dig. He is actually good fun to bowl to because he'll take up the challenge. It's very aggressive cricket and great for the crowd.

My other memory of that Test relates to Funky Miller. I was fielding at mid-on when he started a spell in the first innings, bowling offies. Halfway through the over when Sinclair got on strike Funky immediately changed to medium pace, and with his first ball he trapped Sinclair lbw with an inswinger. I couldn't believe it. It's hard enough being able to bowl one type of style, let alone two. Funky is so versatile, and a very valuable member of the team. The way he plays the game is also a lesson to us all. He's the best example of someone who takes the game seriously but also knows it has to be fun too.

We won that Test by six wickets and the next stop was Hamilton for the final Test. It was another six-wicket win, giving us a clean sweep of the series. I took 5–77 and 3–46. It was very satisfying finishing with 'five-for'. I'd started the season with a bag, and finished the season with a bag.

Everything seemed to go my way in that Test, especially when I was bowling to Craig McMillan in the first innings. He was batting really well, and I can honestly say I wasn't sure how I was going to get him out.

Michael Slater was at mid-off, and as I was walking back to my mark he and I had a bit of joke and chat that went like this:

'Come on Bing, hit me with a wicket.'
'What, this ball?'
'Yeh, this ball.'
'What do you want?'
'Give me a nick.'
'OK. I'll bowl this wide of the crease, swing one out, and see if he'll go for it.'

So in I went, I jumped wide, threw the ball well out, and I couldn't believe it when McMillan poked at it and nicked it through to Gilly. Instead of running towards the keeper and slips cordon, which is the normal thing to do, I turned straight to Slats and we were laughing our heads off. Our light-hearted plan had come off. It was my lucky day.

It wrapped up a great tour for me, but there was one negative moment that really annoyed me, which was at Hamilton in the warm-up game against Northern Districts before the Tests began. I was reported by umpire Dave Quested for running through the crease and trying to hurt their number 11 batsman Bruce Martin in the final over of the first day. It basically implied that I was cheating. There's no doubt I was trying to intimidate the batsman with the ball in question. I was trying to bowl really quickly and bounce him, get the ball up into his ribs and make it uncomfortable. When most bowlers go over the crease, they are trying for that extra bit of pace. Most no-balls are only marginal, no more than half an inch to an inch, but I got my run-up so wrong on this occasion that I overstepped the mark by nearly a foot. Because the pitch was quite soft I could see my sprig marks. I couldn't believe it. I immediately thought that the mark must have been left by my first follow-through footstep. I was really surprised. But then as I was walking back the umpire said, 'That's *your warning. You are trying to intimidate the batsman.' I told him I hadn't done it on purpose and I apologised.*

At the end of the day Quested went back out onto the field with a tape measure to see how far over I was. To make matters worse he measured the distance from my back sprig, which added about another half-inch to the distance. He told the media, but I wasn't allowed to comment. The whole incident was badly exaggerated. It was an honest mistake, and after the match I apologised to Martin. He was OK about it, and accepted what had happened. I was very disappointed because my sportsmanship had been questioned. Playing the game fairly is something I'm very conscious of, and I never want to be considered as someone who abuses the game. Hopefully it will never happen again.

For Brett, the incident was a small blemish on a very rewarding tour. He finished the Test series with 18 wickets at 17.50, giving him the staggering haul of 31 wickets at 16.09 from just five Tests. The PricewaterhouseCoopers ratings system ranked cricket's newest sensation as the sixth-best bowler in the world behind Shaun Pollock, Glenn McGrath, Allan Donald, Curtly Ambrose and Muttiah Muralitharan. Such rankings were subject to cold statistical analysis but, whether Brett's performances were determined by scorebooks or critical eyes, it was obvious that Australia had unearthed a rare find. Dennis Lillee's comparison of Brett with previous pacemen was testimony to that:

At that stage he was on his way to becoming one of the most exciting fast bowlers we'd ever seen. I'd no doubt about that.

It's a great feeling to be able to bowl at extreme pace. Brett has that, and his performance over the summer certainly rekindled memories of the '70s when there were all the West Indian bowlers and a few quick Australians. Back then, it was a real contest of pace and nerve.

I would have loved the chance to have bowled with Brett. He'd be similar to being at the other end to Thommo. The only thing is that Brett is a lot more accurate than Thommo. I'm sure Thommo won't mind me saying that because being more erratic does have its advantages. With Thommo, there were times when he didn't quite get the ball on line, but it would jag back from outside the off-stump to nearly cut the batsman in half. Unpredictability is sometimes a great thing.

But there's no doubt they have something in common. And that is pace. I think you'll find Thommo never ever worried about how fast he was bowling. He ran in and just basically let the ball go. I haven't actually spoken to Brett about this, but if I did, one piece of advice I would give him is to say, 'Don't worry about how fast you're bowling because it's fast enough. Whether it's 95 miles an hour or 100, it's still bloody quick.'

You have to be very mentally strong to bowl fast. It's not something for the weak-minded or weak-bodied. It's very strenuous, tough, and uncompromising at times. Brett knows all that, he loves the challenge of it all, he has a big heart, and I've no doubt those characteristics will take him a long way. All he has to do is stay fit, keep his head, keep working hard on his game and not relax. If he does all that, we are going to see something very special in years to come.

It took just two weeks after the New Zealand tour for something special to occur. Australia was playing the last of three limited-over matches in South Africa when Brett delivered a series of thunderbolts at Johannesburg's Wanderers Stadium. Two balls were clocked at 156 kilometres an hour, the fastest recorded since Jeff Thomson had nudged 160 kilometres — 100 miles an hour on the old scale — in the 1970s.

Brett says:

That day I wasn't trying to bowl fast. Some of the most respected bowlers of all time, including Alan Davidson and Dennis Lillee, had told me that if I wanted to bowl my quickest, I had to attack the crease but maintain a relaxed action.

That day I was bowling with the brand new white ball, and felt very comfortable. The breeze was slightly against me, and was helping my outswinger. The first ball I bowled flashed up on the scoreboard as 146 kilometres an hour, and I thought, 'Geez that's pretty quick for a warm up!' The next ball the crowd yelled, and I looked up to see I'd clocked 152. I bowled a few other balls up around the same mark, and peaked at 156 against Jonty Rhodes and Mark Boucher. I thought about having a crack at the 100-mile mark, but line and length were more important. If I bowled quicker I would have been happy, but not at the expense of my accuracy.

I suppose it does mean a lot to me to reach the 100-mile barrier, and one day everything might be so much in my favour that I will be able to have a real crack at the mark. But if it never happens, it won't worry me.

Brett took 3–32 off 10 overs, but his efforts weren't enough to save Australia from a four-wicket defeat and a 2–1 loss in the series. Shane finished wicket-less in the same match, and neither brother reached double figures when batting. In the two earlier games, Brett had taken 2–57 and 3–32. Shane played only one other encounter, claiming 2 for 19 and scoring 8.

While the South Africans took great pride in avenging their World Cup defeat, the series was overshadowed by one of the biggest scandals in cricket history. The night before Australia left for the short tour, news broke that Indian police had taped phone conversations of South African captain Hansie Cronje allegedly talking with an Indian bookmaker about deals to be made on cricket matches involving South Africa. Cronje was promptly sacked as captain, and stood down from the series with Australia.

Shane says:

When the news broke, we all talked about it. I just couldn't believe that Hansie could have been involved with it. Then I thought maybe he'd just been naive like Mark Waugh and Shane Warne when they gave out information on certain things. Maybe he was just plain stupid and greedy. Whatever he'd done, I thought he'd taken one hell of a risk because not only was he damaging cricket's reputation and his own image, but once you get involved with those sorts of guys you just don't know what can happen.

Death threats against yourself? Or your family? No matter what the financial gains, who'd want personal safety hanging over their head?

We left Australia not knowing exactly how bad the allegations were. But by the time we arrived in South Africa it was huge news. It was front page on all the papers, and everywhere you turned there was something on a news bulletin or people would be talking about it. We tried to steer away from the issue throughout the series, but there was one thing that caught our attention. Herschelle Gibbs had a really bad series with the bat and, although I can't remember who it was, one of our guys said he wouldn't be surprised if Herschelle's poor form meant he had other things on his mind and was somehow involved with Hansie. And so it proved.

The whole betting scandal was very sad. Cricket has always had a lot of credibility from its tradition, but a couple of greedy guys destroyed a lot of the game's image. There's no doubt it will take time to rebuild it, but cricket will recover. It's a game of great character and great characters.

Although the match-fixing issue became one of the most damaging incidents in cricket's history, there was another controversy about to break. And Brett would find himself right in the middle of it.

CHAPTER FOURTEEN

A KINK IN BRETT'S ARMOURY

*There were NO COMPLAINTS from the Aussie Camp
when the Warne/Waugh Bookie Scandal was concealed
from the international cricket community for a whopping
four years (48 months) ... The Aussies were happy that
the dirt was swept under the carpet. When there was just
a 3 month delay in reporting the Brett Lee chucking saga,
the Aussie camp is unhappy with the ICC.
This is sheer hypocracy [sic] ... Think about it
Brett when you next go to a restaurant [sic] it is now
your turn 'cos the Waiter/Waitress will come up to you
(To take your order) & say:
'Now what would the chucker like to order'*
Anonymous e-mail sent to Brett, July 2000

Chucking is one of the most emotive and controversial issues in cricket. In recent times Sri Lanka's rubber–wristed off–spinner Muttiah Muralitharan and Pakistan's Rawalpindi 'Express' Shoaib Akhtar have both suffered the ignominy of being labelled chuckers. Australia's most infamous victim was left–arm paceman Ian Meckiff, who played 18 Tests in the late 1950s and early 1960s before he was no-balled out of the game. In his autobiography, *Thrown Out*, he described in simple but telling terms what it was like to be cursed with a suspicious action:

> No longer could I go out and play cricket for the sheer enjoyment of it. Now, every time I bowled I was conscious that everybody was watching me, waiting for me to make the slightest mistake. It was like being thrown into the sea when you are unable to swim.

Four decades later, it was Brett's turn to keep his head above water after his action was questioned by Indian umpires Srinivas Venkataraghavan and Arani Jayaprakash during the First and Third Tests of Australia's tour of New Zealand. Their concerns were reported to the International Cricket Council by match referee Mike Denness. What followed was a long and painful process that not only put Brett in the spotlight, but also did nothing to enhance the ICC's already battered reputation. It took the ICC three months to inform the Australian Cricket Board that Brett had been reported, prompting Steve Waugh to react in typically dry fashion: 'At least I can say they [the ICC] are consistent.'

Speculation about Brett's bowling first surfaced during India's tour game against New South Wales at the Sydney Cricket Ground in December 1999. It was little more than three weeks before Brett would launch his Test career, and coach Kapil Dev was quietly ensuring the media knew there was concern about Australia's fast-rising star. Dev requested footage of Brett, and within a few days the issue had erupted into a main story in Indian newspapers and on the Internet. It was further fuelled by anonymous quotes from Indian players.

Brett remembers:

I knew there was a whisper going around during that match that Kapil wasn't happy. He apparently thought a few balls I bowled were pretty suspect. The guys in the NSW team said I had nothing to worry about, so I kept bowling. Then all of a sudden accusations started popping up everywhere. Dev didn't comment on what he thought, but the rumours continued right up to my selection in the First Test. I thought it was all over after the Indians had gone home at the end of the summer because I didn't know of anyone else who had any problems with my action.

But it all came out again in July 2000. My immediate reaction was to think that Kapil was probably behind it again. He was the first person to start the whisper, and then I got reported by Indian umpires. It made sense, but who knows.

It was a real roller-coaster ride for me. I'd been in London on a bit of a holiday, and was on top of the world after being named the Young International Cricketer of the Year. Things were happening so fast. I'd only played five Tests and I had to keep telling myself, 'Geez this is really happening. It's not a dream. This is great. I want to enjoy every moment of it.'

But things soon changed. My manager, Neil Maxwell, who was in London with me, found out about the report to the ICC two days before we flew back to Australia. He decided not to tell me until we arrived back home because he wanted me to enjoy the rest of my break.

Once we arrived in Sydney, he told me that we had a two o'clock meeting with Malcolm Speed (ACB Chief Executive) at the SCG. I didn't question why, I just thought it was going to be about contracts.

When we met just before two o'clock, Maxey had this really worried look on his face. I asked him what was wrong, and that's when the truth came out. He said, 'There've been a few problems with you.' I thought, 'Shit what have I done? I've done nothing wrong.' Then he told me about the report. It hit me like a sledgehammer. A few minutes earlier I thought we were going to have a really positive chat about contracts, then all of a sudden everything had turned into a really big negative.

We sat down with Malcolm, who said we had to make the issue public. He told us a media conference would be arranged to talk about everything that was going on — the report, the ACB's views, the possible repercussions. He said we had nothing to hide, so he wanted to get it all out in the open.

After the meeting we had a good chat to Tim May, the head of the Cricketers' Association, and we decided we'd hold the presser [press conference] the following day, Tuesday. We had a briefing about what we were going to say, then I went home. I was so nervous, almost sick, but I kept telling myself that I'd done nothing wrong. My flatmate, Corey Richards, said I looked like a ghost when I walked through the door. For a couple of hours I was totally gone, just walking around not knowing what to think or say.

I was still on edge when Steve Waugh called me up that night. He said, 'I've played with you a fair bit, and as far as I'm concerned you have nothing to worry about. Just don't listen to them. All you have to do is keep taking wickets. Everyone's just jealous.' That really gave me a lift. For the captain of the Australian team to call me up at home nearly put a lump in my throat. It was a weird feeling to think that I'd only played five Tests but was suddenly getting the support of such an important person. For the first time I began to feel positive about it; I refused to think negatively.

The next day Steve, Malcolm, Maxey and I went to the New South Wales Cricket Association offices at lunch time to prepare for the afternoon media conference. Steve and Malcolm stressed again that everyone was behind me. It gave me a lot of confidence, but it was still nerve-racking at the presser. The place was packed. I felt like I'd committed murder and was about to go in front of the jury. There were lights and cameras everywhere, but when I walked in no-one said a word. It was so quiet, the only thing I heard was my heartbeat.

The first few minutes were the toughest I'd ever had in front of the media. This was a new experience because until then I'd always been asked good, positive questions by journalists. I always knew there would be a time when I had to face questions over a form slump or something I'd done wrong, but this was strange because I was being accused of something that I firmly believed I wasn't guilty of.

When asked about my action I tried to be as positive as I could, saying that I thought my delivery was pure, and I was shocked and disappointed in what was happening. I also spoke about how I was unable to fully straighten my arm since breaking it years earlier at the Australian Under-17 carnival in Tasmania.

Looking back, I shouldn't have worried about the questions because it seemed that the media were all behind me, and they didn't actually ask me that much. Steve and Malcolm seemed to be in the firing line just as much. They handled all the tougher questions about the whole process of reporting, and how slow the ICC had been.

I can't remember how long the presser went for. Maybe it was half an hour, maybe longer, but I do know I was really glad when it was over. I felt relieved and pretty happy because I thought everything had gone well. My most important aim was to give the impression that I didn't doubt myself because that would have bred doubt in others. Thankfully the papers the next day were all very fair. All I could do now was wait for the ICC's official hearing into my action three weeks later.

Those three weeks were the hardest of my life, but they were made easier by the amazing amount of support around me. I received heaps of letters, not only from Australians but from Indians and Pakistanis as well. Many stressed that they liked my bowling because it was fast and exciting to watch. I even came home one night after band practice, turned on the television, and there was John Howard saying he supported me. I thought, 'Gee, if I've got the Prime Minister behind me, then I'm doing OK.'

I also had people stopping me in the streets of Sydney and Wollongong, offering their support by saying things like: 'Stuff the umpires mate, you're no chucker!' And then there was the late night call from England. It was about eleven o'clock and I was just about to go to bed when the phone rang. It was Warney, who'd been in the middle of his own controversy with the phone-sex scandal. I asked him what had been happening and he joked, 'Where do I start?'

It was a funny conversation at first, but then he became serious and told me not to listen to what all the accusers were saying. He said it was just a way to cut down the tall poppy. I really appreciated his support.

By the time the hearing came around at the ACB's offices in Melbourne I was comfortable with my position, but I knew the biggest test was to come. It was August the first — I'll never forget the date. The ICC had arranged a telephone hook-up involving the 10 members of its

Advisory Panel on Illegal Deliveries. I was represented by Neil Maxwell, Malcolm Speed, Tim May, and Dennis Lillee, who was my expert witness.

We had about a 90-minute briefing before the hearing. That really helped to settle my nerves. Dennis was especially confident and assured me, 'If anyone tries to bring you down, I'll blow them out of the water. Mate, your action is pure.'

But I still found it hard to hide my nerves. I was about to be trialled in front of people I didn't even know. Sunil Gavaskar was the panel chairman, and there was a member from each Test-playing nation. Ten men who'd decide my immediate fate, and maybe my future for the next 10 years. There was a part of me that was pretty scared when we first went into the hearing in a little room with a speaker phone sitting in the middle of a table. It was quite intimidating. There was a big whiteboard with each panel member's name written up. The aim was to put a tick or a cross next to each member once they'd given their verdict. To be cleared, I needed six members to support me.

All the members had been given about a week and a half to study five overs of tape which had been taken from the New Zealand games in question. Each member spoke in turn; some of them asked me what I thought of my action. I simply replied that I was confident I had no problem.

Some of the questions needed a bit more thought. I was asked a couple of times why I'd changed my action from side on to front on, and everyone seemed satisfied when I said it was purely a matter of injury prevention. I was also asked if I thought I needed to take the ball up straighter during my delivery action, or should I take it out wider. That's when Dennis jumped in with a perfect five-minute burst that basically destroyed any doubters. I was very, very grateful that he was there.

It seemed to be going really well. Every time we thought we gained the support of a member, I felt more relieved as I watched more ticks going up on the whiteboard. But there were a couple of members who said they weren't sure if I chucked a few deliveries or not. None of them though could say for sure. Whenever there was uncertainty my whole mood would sink and I'd wonder, 'Is this is it? Is this the end?'

At the end of an hour-long hook-up we had to go off line while the panel made its decision. During that time I just stayed in the room and chatted to Maxey. I was confident, but still really nervous. I'd obviously thought about the chance that I'd be asked to do remedial work, and it did worry me. An action is very hard to change if you've pretty well been doing it all your life. But I kept telling myself it wouldn't happen.

Fifteen minutes later, Malcolm Speed answered the most awaited phone call of my life. It was a short call, and Malcolm couldn't hide his smile. I'd been cleared by all 10 members. What a relief. I just felt a huge weight lift off me, and it didn't take long for everyone in the room to crack open a beer. My next goal was to get ready for the Indoor Series against South Africa in Melbourne a fortnight later. It was great to finally be thinking about cricket again with a clear head.

The whole issue could have been handled much better. The ICC should have had access to more footage from a wider variety of angles, and if a bowler is to be punished it has to be blatantly obvious that there is a chink in the action. Look at what happened to Shoaib Akhtar. I personally don't have a problem with his action. I think he's fantastic for cricket because things happen when he's playing. He gets bums on seats and packs the stadium. Fans want to watch players like him, and yet there are people who want him banned. I can't work it out.

The hearing itself could also have been improved. If there is going to be a formal examination of a bowler's action, everyone involved should be in the same room. It's easier to communicate when you're face to face with someone, especially when you're trying to explain technicalities. And when you can be deciding a player's future, the playing deserves nothing less. A telephone hook-up is not a fair way to do it at all.

Finally, if I was an umpire who had a problem with a bowler's action, I'd go straight to team management at the end of the day and tell them. To wait three months without knowing is crazy.

The Lee chucking controversy prompted Malcolm Speed to push the ICC for change. The ACB chief executive proposed that the Advisory Panel be cut to just four former players or umpires who'd meet in person with the accused bowler and a representative of the bowler's home board. Together with a qualified biomechanics expert, they would discuss and analyse extensive video footage before making any decisions.

Lillee believes the type of footage shown is critical:

Technology has gone so far ahead that when actions are slowed down at different angles, it would be easy to raise questions over many bowlers who've never been considered suspect over the last 100 years.

To assess any bowler, there has to be simultaneous camera shots from side on, behind and in front. And it should be determined what type of delivery is being bowled: outswinger, inswinger, leg cutter, off cutter, slower ball. It has to be noted that the body angle and wrist movement are different in every delivery. Wrist rotation is an issue that must always be strongly considered.

You have to remember nowadays you're playing with millions of dollars. This is not for the amateurs. It is about people's careers. You'd want to be bloody right.

Just days before Brett became aware that he'd been reported, the ICC had discussed changes to the procedure during its annual meeting in London, but nothing was agreed upon. Afterwards, there was speculation in the Australian media that the ICC moved so slowly in handling the controversy because it had been waiting to see if changes would be made. The whole laborious process prompted Neil Maxwell to consider legal action against the ICC had the decision not been favourable. If Brett had been forced to undertake remedial work after the eventual hearing in August, his participation in Australia's home series against the West Indies would have been in considerable doubt. This would have meant lost time, and undoubtedly lost income for one of the most marketable stars in Australian sport.

Thankfully, no such strategy was needed, and the last lines in the affair were written the day after the hearing when the ACB offices received a huge food and wine hamper from Brett. Brett admits:

It was Maxey's idea. We tend to forget, but there's nothing wrong with athletes getting on with administrators or officials or umpires or referees. After chatting with Maxey, we thought the hamper would be a nice gesture to show my appreciation to Malcolm Speed and the ACB for what they'd done. They looked after me, and were so professional the way they handled the whole affair. I was so grateful for their support. Hopefully we'll never have to go through it again.

★ ★ ★

Just a fortnight before Brett faced the most controversial moment of his career, Shane was floating with news of much better fortunes. In a quiet discussion with the New South Wales coach Steve Rixon, he was told he'd be replacing Michael Bevan as the Blues' captain for the 2000–01 season. He would become the state's 100th leader, and assume a new level of responsibility that was far removed from the party-boy image he had carried with him for much of his career. It was just what Shane needed to dispel former Test cricketer Kerry O'Keefe's comment that, 'Tasmania's batsmen chase as hard as Shane Lee at one o'clock in the morning.'

Shane recalls:

When Steve called me into his office, I thought it was going to be about my stats for last season: it hadn't been a very good year, and I expected to be given a pretty tough time. But it didn't turn out that way at all. I walked out of the office really excited for the future. It was a real honour to be captain. I thought of some of the other players who'd been there before me. Bradman, Benaud, Taylor. It was embarrassing to be in the same list. But I left Stumpa's office confident the captaincy would improve my game. When you're the boss, you have no choice but to lead from the front because there is simply no place to hide.

It was going to mean some changes for me. I knew I'd have to divorce myself from the team a bit. I've always enjoyed being one of the lads, but there'd be times when I'd have to tell them if they stepped out of line. It simply meant I had to be more responsible.

Presenting a responsible image had become an important part of my game both on and off the field. In the previous couple of seasons I'd really worked hard on that. When I first started out in State cricket, I was swept away by part of the New South Wales culture with guys like Greg Matthews and Wayne Holdsworth. They played good hard cricket, but they also enjoyed a party as well. And I suppose I developed a reputation as being a good party-goer: go out until late and get up early for cricket.

I was naive and stupid back then, and that cost me because reputations die hard. If I had my time again I would have certainly kept more to myself in those early days. I've never done anything to jeopardise my cricket, but a couple of big nights here or there can leave lasting impressions.

Kerry O'Keefe's comment really woke me up to that fact. It shook me because perception is everything. I was really annoyed because it was at the stage that I was very conscious of my image. I was training my arse off, doing all the right things, and yet I was being judged on the past.

In the warm-up months to the 2000–01 season I was determined not to put a foot wrong, and when I found out I was going to be captain I tried even harder. I cut back on the band commitments because I didn't want to give the impression that I was out enjoying pub life and having fun when in fact I really had my head down at training. No matter how innocent, I just didn't want to be seen doing the wrong thing. Sure, I still had a few beers here and there, but I was going to make sure I was seen doing the right thing when it counted. It wasn't worth the risk to do anything else.

The first sign of Shane's added responsibility came at the media conference to officially announce the captaincy change in late July. In a novel move, officials decided Shane would be in charge of the conference that would also see the unveiling of a new three-year sponsorship deal for the Blues with the Excell Corporation. So, the media had the unusual sight of Shane welcoming everyone, then

Brett celebrates a wicket with Adam Gilchrist, Shane Warne and Mark Waugh.

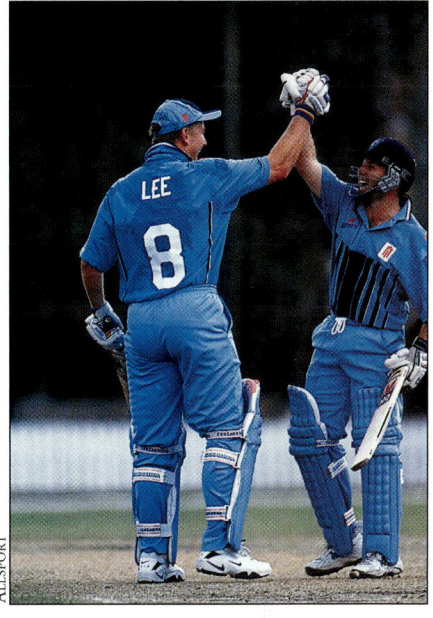

Jackpot! Shane celebrates with Rod Davison after hitting the 90-thousand-dollar target in a Mercantile Mutual Cup match against the ACT.

Shane has spent more than his share of time on the outer.

Whether it be the first or last over of the day, Brett always delivers the same effort.

Reaching for the stars. Brett's trademark leap during Australia's Indoor Series against South Africa at Colonial Stadium in August 2000.

Shane claims a wicket during the drawn one-day series in the Caribbean in 1999.

Brett with Australian Cricketers' Association's Tim May, after being named Australia's Rookie of the Year in 1999–2000.

Surf's up. Although the Lee boys were raised close to some of the best beaches in Australia, cricket was always number one.

Shane in control at the crease for Australia.

Shane is renowned as one of the biggest and hardest hitters in Australian cricket.

A long way from Mount Warrigal. Brett and Shane fulfill a childhood dream of playing for Australia together (1999–2000).

Shane in NSW colours.

'All I want for Christmas.' Brett with his prized baggy green cap before making his Test debut against India in the 1999 Boxing Day Test.

Five wickets on debut and a stump for the memorabilia collection. Brett relaxes after playing a star role in Australia's 1999 Boxing Day Test win against India.

Shane on the attack during his English
county season with Somerset in 1996.

The Natural. Whatever the sport, Shane
makes it look easy.

'Well done, Bro!' Brett races in to congratulate Shane after the dismissal of Jacques Kallis
during Australia's limited overs tour of South Africa in 2000.

Shane scrambles for his ground during a match against India (1999–2000).

While he may play bass guitar, there's little doubt what Brett would rather have in his hand.

'Mate, we've done it!' A moment to be remembered by the Lee family for years to come.
Shane takes a catch off Brett's bowling.

introducing the chairman of the New South Wales Cricket Association, Bob Horsell, to make a 'special announcement'. Horsell promptly announced Shane as captain, and allowed the new leader to continue proceedings. Both the captaincy and sponsorship announcement were somewhat overshadowed by the appearance of Mark Waugh, who faced a constant stream of questions over a television report into match-fixing that was broadcast two days earlier on the ABC's 'Four Corners' program. Did Waugh have anything to hide? Was he willing to make his financial records available to investigators? What was his reaction to former Pakistan captain Imran Khan claiming that there may have been further Australian involvement in match-fixing?

In comparison, the questions asked of Shane were much tamer, the most obvious of which was: 'Could NSW improve on its dismal record of recent seasons?'

'I think we can,' were among the first words he uttered in his new role. 'We've got a pretty good structure in place. We've got Steve Rixon back on board, a proven coach both domestically and internationally. We've got a full-time manager of the team in David Sincock. So there's a very professional approach. With discipline and learning from the mistakes of the past, there's no reason why we can't be successful this year.' And of his predecessor, who was away at the time, Shane says:

My appointment was helped by Bevo's reaction. He was in England at the time playing county cricket, but we had a good chat when he came back for Australia's pre-season camp in Queensland. I don't know whether he felt there was a bit of weight lifted off his shoulders, which would allow him to put more into his batting again. Whether he was captain or not, I was hopeful he'd play a big role. I certainly hoped to take a lot of advice from him.

Shane had gained his first senior captaincy role with Campbelltown, whose 1994–95 annual report was full of praise for its then 21-year-old leader:

Our club captain had another extraordinary year with the bat, almost treating grade bowling with contempt. He must surely play for Australia in the very near future. His leadership qualities are excellent and his tactical work as captain is improving with experience, who is to say that he will not one day lead his country.

However, it wasn't until his role as stand-in skipper against Queensland early in the 1999–2000 season that he showed how he relished the added responsibilities at an interstate level. Later that season he enhanced his reputation as a strong leader when he steered the Australian 'A's to two victories against Pakistan. Shane acknowledges:

Captaincy really keeps me alert. Mark Taylor told me after the Brisbane games that I obviously played better when I was captain. So, he suggested when I wasn't captain I still had to take a leadership approach into my game. I tried that throughout Australia's 1999–2000 one-day series, and it definitely worked for me. It was really good advice. Now at State level I don't have to pretend. There's no doubt captaincy needs a different mind-set. It's basically about man management, getting the best out of the players all the time.

It was going to be one of the toughest jobs of his career: helping to resurrect a cricket-proud state that had fallen on tough times.

CHAPTER FIFTEEN

THE WINTER GAME

*Cricket is about entertaining. Every player has
to remember they are there to obviously play to their
best ability, but also put on a good show. It will
become more important in the future. We have to
move with the times.*

Shane Lee

In addition to the chucking dramas that interrupted his 2000 winter, Brett underwent surgery to fix his ankle problems. His recuperation process involved early morning sand runs along Balmoral beach in Sydney's inner north. By the time he'd recovered, Australia was ready for an innovative three-match series against South Africa at Melbourne's indoor Colonial Stadium.

Brett says:

Everyone was really looking forward to it. Apart from some of the guys who'd gone over to play county cricket, the series was the first hit-out for most of our players in four months. It was good to be involved in something new and different. It felt a bit weird though to be playing cricket during footy season. It was only August, and still pretty cold. And it was really different playing under a closed roof. At first, I kept looking up and expected to see stars. It took a little bit of getting used to. It was actually a bit like having jet lag because we'd drive to the ground in broad daylight, then all of a sudden we'd be in darkness inside the stadium. The change played a few mental tricks on me, and there were times during matches when I didn't know whether it was night or day, and whether I should feel tired or wide awake. I felt like an owl.

The matches were full of hype. Each player had a theme song to introduce him when he batted or bowled. I chose 'Eye of the Tiger' by Survivor. I know it was a pretty old tune, but it did pump me up. I must still be living in the '80s!

Overall, though, I thought it was a really good concept. The fact that they had music, lighting and sound right around the ground created a great atmosphere. The pitch had been prepared elsewhere, and was only dropped in a few days before the series began. It played pretty well. It was hard and bouncy at first and, although it slowed up in the last couple of games, there were no surprises with it.

But the outfield was far too wet. Many fieldsman were slipping and sliding, and constantly scraping mud off their spikes. That made it a little bit dangerous for me since the opening game was my first since coming back from ankle surgery. So I didn't bowl flat chat. But I felt much better by the last game, and started to get a lot more grip and gave myself more of a workout.

The series was drawn, with each team winning one game, and in a repeat of the World Cup they also tied a match. Brett took three wickets in two matches, while Shane claimed two scalps and tallied 40 runs from two innings, the highlight of which was 28 off just 15 deliveries, including two cover-driven sixes off Shaun Pollock in the series opener. Shane remembers:

I came in right near the end of the innings. Bevo and Tugga [Steve Waugh] had both scored hundreds. Bevo had just got out, but Tugga was still there. It was quite funny when he met me in the middle. He told me his legs were absolutely stuffed and the less running we had to do the better. He said, 'Back yourself, try to get a few boundaries.' Then when I hit the sixes off Pollock, he came up to me and said, 'Keep going mate. I can hardly move!' It was a good feeling. I suppose I'd left my own little mark on history by being the first batsman to hit a six indoors, but it didn't mean anything to me.

The series was good fun. I chose an even less modern song than Brett — 'Prisoner of Society'. The guys didn't mind all the hype and glitz. They could see what the ACB was trying to do. Obviously it was a chance to experiment and test the waters about adding another dimension to cricket. I think it worked pretty well.

It was a good stadium, but I'm not sure whether games in winter are the best idea. Perhaps the way to go is to keep playing in summer, have the roof open when it's sunny, but close it when it looks like raining. I don't think Test cricket under a roof is that far away at all.

The limited-overs game is the perfect place to trial new things. Just before the indoor series, all of Australia's contracted players had a training camp in Queensland. And we took some of the ideas from that camp into the Colonial Stadium matches.

Throughout the camp we were just trying to take things to a new level. For the first time we tried to incorporate set moves into our game plan like they do in rugby. For instance, we had a set move for opener Gary Kirsten where we'd stack the off-side field, bowl one short and wide outside off-stump, and try to get him to smack one straight to the field. If he kept doing it, we'd hope he'd get frustrated because we were trying to cut off his strength.

We called another move 'Roy Orbison', which meant lifting the pressure. When we sensed a batsman couldn't get off strike and was getting a little edgy, all the field would move in that little bit for a run-out. The mid-off or mid-on would run straight to the bowler's end after every delivery in case the batsmen did try to take a quick single. It's not rocket science, and we were in fact only doing the things we'd always do, but we were continually trying to increase the awareness.

It's part of John Buchanan's influence. He is always trying to look for something that little bit different. The moves didn't work during the games, but I think you'll see more of that type of stuff down the track.

Brett agrees Australia's approach is changing under Buchanan and Steve Waugh:

The first time I met Buck [John Buchanan] I thought he looked like a basketball coach. I don't know what it was, but he had a book under one arm and a really switched-on manner. He always has the whole training session planned out. There are heaps of coaches who'll just say, 'OK we'll bowl for 40 minutes, then have a fielding session, and that'll be it.' Whereas Buck will say, 'We'll bowl for 40 minutes, then the bowlers will do 50 catches left- and right-handed.' He has every activity set out over a three-hour period. He knows exactly what he wants to get from the players. He loves having one-on-one chats, and he keeps drumming in our ears that if we're going to improve we have to keep going outside the boundaries of ordinary thinking. That's why we tried a few things differently during the indoor matches.

There are heaps of guys who could get comfortable doing the same thing all the time, doing no more than just batting or bowling in the nets. But that's what Buck has been trying to get us out of the habit of doing. There are always new ways and new techniques to improve our game.

He is very analytical. He puts down each ball that's bowled, then at the end of the game he analyses all the individual performances. For example, he might look at the twenty-third over, which might be the final over in a five-over spell for me. He'll see that my fourth and fifth deliveries were both cut for four, and the last ball was clipped away off the batsman's legs for two. He'll then come back to me and say, 'OK, I can see when you were getting a bit tired. You probably should have had a rest by then.'

He has got some long-term goals, which have been placed in a pyramid style. Every series or achievement is a step up towards the peak, which is the 2003 World Cup. He makes us sort out our team goals, and once we walk onto the field it has been drummed into us that we can't let any of our mates down.

A month after the indoor series there was a really positive feeling in the side when we went over to Kenya for the ICC knockout tournament. Although it didn't prove to be a successful trip, we called it the 'Wild Dog tour'. Before the tournament began the team went through a game park, and were told about wild dogs that hunted in packs. It was what we were trying to achieve, everyone working together. Unfortunately we were more like puppy dogs on that tour, but the thoughts of who we were and what we could achieve remained with us.

It ended up being a disappointing tournament because India knocked us out in the quarter-finals. We got off to a pretty bad start in the match when Pidgey [Glenn McGrath] was being caned around the ground by Tendulkar. I eventually picked him up, caught by Damien Martyn in the slips, but the rest of the batsmen did well enough to reach 265 on a small ground. Shane and I both took two wickets, but the team was penalised two overs for slow over rates. After all we'd talked about in the pre-season camp about being professional and on top of our game, we just weren't as focused as we should have been. We lost by 20 runs, and one of the few memorable parts of my performance was my batting. After a reasonable start we lost a few quick wickets, including Shane for one, then the next thing you know I'm out there batting with Tugga for the first time. He was amazing because of the amount of confidence he gave me. He said, 'This ground is too small for you. You can hit anyone out of the park.' He was trying to get me all fired up, but he also told me to stick to the basics. After a couple of overs I started picking the ball up pretty well, and Steve kept encouraging me, telling me that once the ball was up I shouldn't be frightened to go for a hit. And when their left-armer Zaheer Khan put one in the slot, I had to have a go at it. It left the bat sweetly and went sailing out of the ground, and smashed a car window. It felt great. One of the sweetest shots I'd ever played. Every good shot stands out for a bowler because we don't get the chance to play many! Unfortunately we lost Steve, and our chase all went downhill from there. I made 31 before Ajit Agarkar got me. After the World Cup a lot of people expected us to do better, but it was a very good learning curve for us. We'd been on top, but it just proved how easy it was to be knocked off. It was an important kick up the backside heading into the new season against the West Indies.

CHAPTER SIXTEEN

THE DOMINATORS

*In addressing the Australian side before the Test series,
Steve Waugh spoke about us becoming a tougher side.
He said we weren't going to play good cricket against the
West Indies, we were going to play 'excellent cricket'.
He said if we got the Windies by the throat, then we'd
really have to go in and nail them.*

Brett Lee

The 2000–01 season was much awaited by Brett, who was entering his first complete top-class season at home. He warmed up with an impressive 5–42 against Victoria at Melbourne's Punt Road Oval in the Blues' first Pura Cup match for the season. At full strength NSW won by 117 runs, a perfect start under the coaching of the state's prodigal son, Steve Rixon.

Brett played only one more Pura Cup game and five Mercantile Mutual one-dayers before turning his attention to the five-Test series against the West Indies. There was no doubt he'd be selected for the First Test, and if he maintained the standard set in his five matches the previous season a golden summer loomed. His team-mates and the public were also anticipating a memorable series against the West Indies. Having won 10 Tests in a row, Australia was just one match away from equalling the world record set by Clive Lloyd's brilliant team of the early 1980s.

Brett says:

Heading into the Test Tugga [Steve Waugh] said we were good enough to beat the record, but he stressed we needed to stick to the basics first. It was just a case of doing well at the Gabba, then taking it from there. He didn't want to put too much pressure on us — apart from the pressure of playing better cricket. But I could tell that the record would be something special for Tugga. He loves the historical side of cricket, loves to break records, and loves to set new marks for the team to achieve.

There was a different type of feeling for me entering this Test. Last time I came into the squad halfway through the summer, but this time it was a brand new start. It was a huge feeling to be chosen because I knew I had a chance to play the whole summer. It was a real buzz, especially because we were playing the West Indies. I'd watched them on TV when I was a kid, and there was a real aura surrounding them. I dreamt of one day coming in and firing up like their fast bowlers used to do. Now, I was about to do just that. I kept telling myself, 'Geez, you're doing this for real. You're really doing this. Can you believe it?' I was very excited. It was a great honour and thrill.

There was a lot of talk about the pitch. The curator Kevin Mitchell said he didn't think it would bounce as much as a lot of people thought. When I first saw it, it had a lot of grass on it. Then out came the ground staff and cut it all off. Pidgey [Glenn McGrath] and I had a laugh about that. It seems to happen the world over for fast bowlers!

We won the toss and Tugga was convinced there would be something in it for us, so he sent the Windies in. Walking out onto the field, it was interesting watching the other guys. Everyone was so excited about playing. Most of us had had a really good rest over the winter, and were really ready to go. I'd never seen a keener bunch of blokes.

I was never nervous going into that match, but I was anxious. I just wanted to get into playing again, and hopefully to continue what I'd done the previous summer. I wanted to show everyone that I wasn't a 'one summer wonder'. Tugga played an important role in that. He is an amazing person to play with, especially when it comes down to field placings. Nine times out of ten he accepts what the bowler wants. If I ever wanted to have six slips and two gullys, Tugga would actually do it. He gives the bowlers a lot of support. If he thinks the bowler feels very confident about setting the fields, he puts the responsibility on the bowler. I know when he does that with me, the biggest thing in my mind is not to let Tugga down and to prove to him I know what I'm doing. I've never been knocked back by him for a field placing. Sometimes I haven't been right and things don't work, but at least I'm allowed to try.

At the start of my first spell in Brisbane, he was short and sweet. He said he wanted me to go and bowl four or five of the quickest overs I could, and see if I could shake the Windies up with a couple of early wickets. Generally against sides like the Windies, who hadn't been playing good cricket in the lead up, we knew getting a quick breakthrough could give us another couple of wickets almost straight away.

Steve threw me the ball, and we agreed on the field placings. He said, 'Just stick to a good line and length. Don't overdo the bouncer. I'll give you three slips, a gully, and a third man for the flier. Good luck.' And away I went.

The ball didn't carry through a hell of a lot in the opening session, but I felt quite good about the way I was bowling. I had a real scare in my first spell when I slipped during my delivery stride and landed on my right ankle. It could have been quite dangerous, and it actually scared me a bit because it made me realise how accidents can happen so quickly and when you're least expecting them. I could have snapped an ankle or torn a groin. I also felt something go in my back, but I just thought it was a bit of a muscular twinge from hitting the deck. For a few moments it was hard to put it out of my mind, but after a few more deliveries I was fine again. It did make me wonder though about the fine line that professional sportsman have to walk: an injury can wreck a career in the blink of an eye.

I only got one wicket in the innings, but it was great to be able to watch Pidgey from close range. We rolled the Windies for 82, and Pidgey took

6–17 off 20 overs. It was unbelievable bowling. He just kept bowling in the channel, ball after ball. Channel, channel, channel. The batsmen just kept chasing the balls and nicking them. I learnt so much that day. It just goes to prove that if you bowl good line and length with pace and you remain very patient, things are going to happen for you.

There'd been lots of talk in the lead up about the battle between Pidgey and Brian Lara. Pidgey had even said himself in the papers that he fancied himself against Lara. That might have been a bit of a bait. But come the First Test, Pidgey got him hook, line and sinker — caught by Gilly for a duck. You could tell Pidgey just had Lara completely psyched out with the ball moving away outside off-stump. Justin Langer told me that Brian had actually turned to him at short-leg and said, 'This is no fun any more being out here batting.' It just summed up his state of mind. He was shattered.

It happened again in the second innings, when Brian edged a ball when trying to go for the hook and was out for four. Those couple of cheap dismissals helped set up the whole series for us.

Pidgey ended up taking 4–10 off 13 overs in the second innings to make it 10 for the match. The Windies folded for 124, and we'd won by an innings and 126 runs inside three days. I was lucky enough to get 3–40 off 18 overs in the second dig, and was happy with my first-up effort. I knew there was a lot of improvement, but it was a good start after coming off such a long break.

But my batting was the real surprise. Michael Slater and Matthew Hayden got us away to a really good start in the first innings but we fell away a bit in the middle order, and we were 7–220 by the time I came in to join Gilly. The pitch was starting to keep a little low, and the ball was beginning to jag off a couple of cracks.

Gilly told me just to watch the ball as closely as I could. Our goal was to face 80 balls — we'd actually made that pact before the game when every player signed off on their own achievement contracts. The contracts were just another one of John Buchanan's ideas and were a way of lifting our levels of responsibility. During one mid-wicket chat, Gilly came down to me and said, 'We've gotta do what Buck wants. Remember, 80 balls.'

Facing 80 balls is a big ask for a tailend batsman, but it really made me switch on and believe I could achieve it.

It was Gilly's suggestion that we bat in partnerships of 10. It started slowly at first, then the next thing you know we were hitting 14 an over. I had to scratch around until I made about 20, but then I started feeling a lot more comfortable. I hit a cover-drive in my twenties, and it came right out of the screws. That shot made me feel a lot more comfortable, and all of a sudden I was thinking, 'I'm not going to let these bastards get me out because I've got the green helmet on, I'm playing for Australia. I'm going to take everything they can dish out.' I was really starting to enjoy it.

Gilly got to 48 and then he got a top edge to Mervyn Dillon and was caught behind. We'd put on 61, and Australia was nearly 200 ahead. Then out walks Stuart MacGill. You could call him Robocop because he walks really stiffly and holds the bat like a machine. He came up to me and asked, 'What's happening out here?' And I told him, 'Well, the bowlers have taken the second new rock, it's about 10 overs old, but it's not doing that much. Just watch the ball, and let's see if we can bat in partnerships of 10.' And away we went. MacGilla at first was ducking and didn't look all that happy, but after he smacked a straight drive past Dillon he looked more confident.

We kept on going and were really frustrating the bowlers. I know when the boot is on the other foot how annoying it can be to be held up by tailenders. Late in the partnership I was approaching 50, and I was actually getting quite nervous. By the time I was on 47, I was starting to think too much about it. I was telling myself, 'Geez I'd better be careful here because I might never get this chance again.' Up until that point I'd been too busy thinking about the team score to worry about mine. In a break between overs MacGilla came up to me and told me there was no way he was going to get out until I got my 50. It was only then that I thought, '50! Shit!' The crowd were right behind me, they were cheering every time the bowler came in. I felt my heart going at a million miles an hour, and it wasn't helped by blocking five balls in a row when I was on 49. I just couldn't get a single. Nixon Mclean was bowling pretty short to me, and I was trying to flick one off my ribs. Then I finally pushed a ball to cover and MacGilla just took off, so I thought I'd better go too. Before I knew it, the ball was being thrown to the bowler's end and I knew I was in trouble, and was worried I'd look like a real goose if I was run-out on 49. I took a big dive, the ball went flying past the stumps, and kept on going to the fence for four overthrows. I jumped up and thought, 'Wow, a Test 50. I've made a bloody Test 50. Can you believe it?' It was one of the highlights of my career because every bowler likes getting runs, and every bowler reckons he can bat a bit too. Just ask Pidgey.

Once I'd made the 50, we had a plan to get a few quick runs. I was seeing the ball quite well, but in truth the Windies were bowling really badly to me. They were banging the ball in far too short and wide outside off-stump, giving me heaps of room to cut.

Marlon Black kept slamming all these balls in short, but I knew if he pitched one up I was going to go straight and hard because the mid-off and mid-on were really wide and close, and there was no-one back deep. So I thought the worst thing that could happen if I swung hard was to get a top edge, and with the luck going my way the ball would probably go for six anyway. About three balls later he pitched one up, I had a go at it, and the ball came right off the middle of the bat and away it went. Bang. A six. That was a great feeling. Just as good as getting a wicket.

MacGilla was run out for 19 soon afterwards, but not before we'd put on 50 between us. Pidgey went for a duck, so I finished with 62 not out off 80 balls. I'd lived up to the contract.

I really enjoyed it out there. I'd always dreamt of getting some runs in Test cricket, but not that many. Much of the credit goes to Buck. Apart from helping with the technical side, he has given me tremendous self-belief. Along with Tugga, he is just very, very confident in his players. Even before the Brisbane match he'd been telling me that I could score fifties in Test cricket. I'd just roll my eyes and grin. But then when I did get the 50, I looked over to the dressing room and there was Buck clapping his hands above his head and smiling. He was as happy as I was, he was really sharing in the achievement. He's always the first to training, and the last to leave. He trains us hard, but always fairly.

The contracts aren't the only different things he does. In Brisbane there must have been about six or seven pieces of butcher's paper around the dressing room. Some had messages written by the players, others had particular goals. At any time we could look at them and feel stirred. The key words I'd heard and seen most in the lead up to that Test was 'Never Satisfied'. Not only were they written on a spreadsheet in Brisbane, but in any match Australia plays you can find them underlined or in inverted commas on a piece of paper somewhere in the dressing room.

The win in Brisbane made it 11 victories on the trot. The team had a few celebrations that night, but most of us wanted to wait until after the Second Test in Perth. We had levelled the record of Clive Lloyd's team, but we wanted the mark to ourselves. And if we won at the WACA, then we'd really let our hair down. It was great to get the First Test out of the way, relax for a couple of days then switch on for the big one. Each player knew it.

There was a lot of media hype before the WACA Test. Not only was there talk about us making it to 12 wins, but there was a fair bit of speculation about whether I could break the 160-kilometres-an-hour mark. As soon as I hopped off the plane at Perth, reporters were asking me about my chances. Even fans were coming up to me and saying, 'Here's your best chance of breaking the record because Perth has a really fast pitch.' What people don't realise is that pace is measured through the air, not off the wicket. You can bowl as fast as you want; it should never matter what pitch you're on.

I sat down and had a chat to Buck about all the hype, and we agreed that I just had to keep doing what I had been doing. I played all the hype right down, and that's the way I honestly felt. I wasn't putting on a face or anything like that. My view was that I could bowl line and length around the 140–145 mark, and that was quick enough. If a few balls did start coming out really quickly and my accuracy wasn't suffering, then yeh, I would give it a crack, but I didn't spend much time thinking about it.

The match was everything the team hoped it would be. And it even had more with Pidgey's hat-trick in the first innings. Tugga sent the West Indies in again, and they were out for 196 not long after tea on the first day. They had been 5–22 after Pidgey's hat-trick set us up really well. I'd taken the first wicket, trapping Darren Ganga lbw for a duck. Then it was all Pidgey. He got Sherwin Campbell first up, then in came Brian Lara. I was down at fine-leg, and I had a really strange feeling that something was going to happen on the first ball. It was just one of those weird gut feelings. And the crystal ball was right. Brian got an edge and MacGilla took the catch in the slips after juggling the ball for a while. The dismissal seemed to happen in slow motion for me, but when I saw everyone's arms go up I starting sprinting towards the huddle. It was Pidgey's 300th Test wicket. He couldn't have chosen anyone better to get out.

As I was walking back to fine-leg after the celebrations, someone in the crowd yelled out that we were going to see a hat-trick. While Jimmy Adams was walking in, I tried to think of what Pidgey would bowl. I was backing just a good line and length ball. But it was dug in short, and from my position I thought it must have lobbed off Jimmy's ribs. But when Justin Langer caught it at short-leg, the whole team was celebrating. I did another sprint in again. It was fantastic. I felt so lucky to be part of it, even luckier to think that I was sharing the new ball with Pidgey. What an honour, because Glenn McGrath will go down as one of the world's best bowlers of all time. He deserved a hat-trick. They were the only three wickets he took in the innings. I got 2–52, and Jason Gillespie had 3–46. It was the first time the three of us had bowled together and, just like there'd been a lot of talk about our bid for 12 Test wins and my chances of breaking the 160-mark, there had been a lot of publicity about our three-pronged pace-attack. It was great to see Dizzy [Jason Gillespie] back. He'd had a shocking run with injuries. The poor bastard had done his time, and deserved a few good breaks away from injuries. So we were hoping the Perth match would be the first one in a long line of Tests we would play together.

Australia only had to bat once in Perth, and again I hit the ball pretty well to reach 42 not out in 8 declared for 396. But I probably remember my last training session before the match just as much as the innings. I was feeling pretty confident after my 62 in Brisbane, and thought I could just continue batting the same way. A local net-bowler came in, I went for the slog, and the ball flew off the top edge. Tugga walked past and said, 'Come on Binga, one good score doesn't make you a batsman.' I deserved the kick in the butt, and immediately put my head down because I was too *frightened to step out of line with the boss. No matter where he is, Tugga always seems to know what's going on. He has so many things going on in his mind, but he still manages to watch each and every player. It's like he has about 12 sets of eyes. He's not spying, he's just making sure everyone is doing their job the best they can. He really wants to look after each player, knowing he can help because of his experience. That's why he's so good with the younger guys. And his experience was really beneficial for us against the West Indies because he'd been there when Australia was getting crushed. So it didn't take much for him to remind us that it was our turn to do the crushing.*

We'd got our runs so quickly in Perth that we had a handful of overs at the Windies before the end of the second day. And by stumps they were 2–16. Pidgey and I had a wicket each, and I'd again made the first breakthrough when Dizzy caught Sherwin Campbell at gully. I wished we could have kept playing into the darkness because we had all the momentum. The Windies were shattered. Their body language said it all. Their heads were low and they didn't seem to have any spirit. Because of that, it was no surprise when we went through them for 173 the next day.

Like most things that had happened since my Test debut, things had a habit of falling into place like mini fairy tales. And the last over of the Test was one of them. The Windies were 7–173. The ball was starting to reverse swing, the breeze was coming in and the temperature had dropped down a bit, so it was perfect to bowl. I was in my fifteenth over, but still felt nice and strong. First up I bowled Nixon McLean with an inswinger. The boys came into the huddle and we were all getting a bit excited. We had two wickets to get. Two wickets to go until we were part of history. When Marlon Black came out Tugga asked what I was thinking. Some of the other guys said, 'Bounce him, get stuck into him.' But Tugga said, 'No, keep the ball up. If that doesn't work, we might go around the wicket and intimidate him a bit.' I knew exactly what I was going to bowl — a big inswinging yorker. It couldn't have come out more perfectly, Black missed it, and was cleaned up. I was on a hat-trick for the third time in my Test career! I went flying into the huddle, and was thinking, 'Geez, what a way to create history. Imagine ending it with a hat-trick.' I spoke to Pidgey about it because he was the expert after his first innings hat-trick. He asked me what I was going to do. I told him that if I could have dreamt I was on a hat-trick, 99 times out of a 100 I'd pick Courtney Walsh to bowl to, and I'd reckon I'd get him out a fair share of those 99 times too. In came Courtney, he took leg-stump, and I could see this huge gap. I immediately had this picture in my mind of the stumps being knocked over again with a big inswinger. But I got too anxious and a little carried away. I started running in a bit quicker; I was too rushed. The crowd was really loud and right behind me, but when I let the ball go I knew they'd be disappointed. It didn't come out properly, wobbling across the seam and holding its line about half a foot outside off-stump. Courtney still jumped at it, but missed it. Even if there had been a nick, I doubt if anyone would have heard it above the crowd's noise. I was a bit disappointed. It was the third time I'd been on a hatty but missed out. Then I looked at Pidgey. He had to wait 300 wickets until he got one. A hat-trick in Test cricket isn't something I want, but it would be nice for it to happen at some stage in my career.

As I was walking back for my next ball, I tried to work out what Courtney would be expecting me to do. I guessed he'd be looking for another full one. Justin Langer was at short-leg, and Pidgey was at a wider short-leg. I knew that each time Courtney played a bouncer he jumped right to square-leg. Tugga suggested I give Courtney a nice quick bouncer outside leg-stump to see if he'd walk into it and pop a catch to the slips like he'd done in the First Test. Unfortunately my direction was off. I'd tried to bowl too quickly, and Gilly took the ball well over off-stump. It was a wasted chance. I was really annoyed with myself, but just as I was about to turn around and go back to my mark I looked at Walsh, who had a big smile. His eyes lit up, his whole face was grinning. It honestly looked as though he was having a lot of fun. He knew he was in a hopeless position, so he was just going to have a laugh. I walked back to my mark, looked up at the big screen and saw a shot of Tugga laughing his head off. That was a very special moment for me. Here we were being hard professional cricketers, and yet still finding the place to laugh and enjoy what was happening. That summed up Courtney. There was a time and a place for everything with him.

He survived the next ball with a smile too. I had one delivery to go, and I was desperate to try to finish the match with it. I decided to go back to the inswinging yorker. Once again it came out pretty well and thumped Courtney on the pads. What happened next was just a bit of a blur. It seemed the whole team went up, and when the umpire's finger shot up I had goosebumps everywhere. It wasn't so much of a huddle we got into, it was more like a rugby scrum. We were all hugging each other really tightly and jumping over the top of each other. Everyone was shaking hands and congratulating each other. It was a magical moment. Then Punter started the team song. No-one expected it. It was so spontaneous that I hadn't even collected my hat from the umpire when it started. But there's no doubt there was no better place for it. All of us shouted the words as loud as we could. Not once, but twice. Once we stopped, the whole ground got to its feet and started cheering and clapping. A few journalists asked us afterwards if the song was premeditated, but it definitely wasn't. No-one except Punter knew what was going on. It was simply meant to happen that way. We'd worked so hard to break the record, and everyone acknowledged how much every player had been a part of it. We were all really proud of each other.

We did a victory lap, and as we walked past the Lillee–Marsh end, where I'd been bowling from, the crowd gave us a really big cheer. I knew I was very lucky to have come into the team when I did. I couldn't have asked for my first seven Test matches to have gone any better. As we were walking off Tugga said something that stuck in my mind, 'Binga, enjoy this while you can because at some stage it will stop.'

But I didn't realise it would stop so quickly. At lunch on that last day I started to feel really stiff in the back. I leant over to pick up something in the dressing room, and I felt something grab on the lower left-hand side. It didn't feel right. I went and told Errol Alcott that I felt as though there was something pinching in my lower back. It wasn't a really sharp pain, but just a small level of discomfort. I wasn't worried because of the lack of severe pain.

Some other medical staff came in and had a look, then Errol told me to have an ice bath, do some stretches and see how I pulled up after the game. Just as I was about to go back onto the field, he rubbed some Deep Heat into it and it felt great.

After getting the three wickets in the last over, I felt on top of the world and didn't give my back another thought that night while we were celebrating. But the next morning when I woke up, I was still feeling the same stiffness. There'd been times when I'd woken up with stiffness in my calves, my hammies, or my back, but I knew it was just muscle soreness from bowling. This was different. I told Errol again, and he suggested I go back to Sydney to have a precautionary scan.

Unfortunately the scan showed a faint line going through my L3 veterbra. The specialist didn't want to call it a stress fracture because it hadn't evolved that far, but it was on the verge of turning into one. If you don't know what I'm talking about, just imagine hitting a cement wall with a sledgehammer. A line comes up first, then if you keep hitting the wall it will eventually crack. That was the same thing with the bone. We knew the warning signs were there, so I was advised to have a six-week rest. Hopefully by then the line would have cleared. If I kept playing, it may have been OK because the specialist wasn't sure whether the line was a new one. But it wasn't worth the risk.

The injury was very hard to take. I'd just come off a five-wicket haul in a team that was playing excellent cricket. I was floating, but the results of the scan changed everything. I had a good chat to Errol, Trefor James who was the team doctor, and Pat Farhart who was the NSW physio and back-up for the Australian side. Pat was also a very good friend and knew the history of my other back problems. They all said the same thing — I had no choice but to rest. The six weeks meant I'd miss the rest of the Test series. I was shattered.

The time off gave me a good chance to sit back and reflect on what had happened over the last 12 months. It had been unbelievable. Everything had happened so quickly. But then the roller-coaster ride had hit a low spot. I thought I'd been lucky to have gone as far as I did without dramas. I never wanted it to stop the way it did, but injuries hit most athletes at some stage of their careers so I just had to accept what had happened.

Watching the rest of the Tests on TV was very tough. I watched most of the games, but there were times when I just had to go away and do other things because it was too frustrating to watch the guys from a distance. I really wished I was out there winning with them. It was great to see Dizzy and Andy Bichel come back and do very well. It showed how much depth we had in fast bowling. But it was still hard to accept. I never stopped wishing I was out there playing.

Although it was unrealistic, I was aiming to try to get back in time for the last two Tests in Melbourne and Sydney. But with the series already over by then it was decided there was no use rushing back, especially with a tour of India just around the corner. Tugga spoke to me before the Boxing Day Test, and told me the priority was to be ready for the three Tests in India. He was expecting the pace-attack to play a crucial role, despite the fact that pitches on the subcontinent really helped the spinners. He thought reverse swing was going to be critical, and when combined with a pure pace-barrage he was confident India's batsmen would struggle. It was great to think Tugga had that much faith in his fast bowlers. His opinion had a real influence on me. I was really keen to play again, but there was no way I wanted to jeopardise the chances of helping Australia to win its first series in India for 30 years. If I had come back too soon and injured my back again, I would have felt that I'd let Tugga and Australia down.

So, it was rest, rest, and more rest for the first three weeks after the injury. No swimming, no running, no stomach work. Nothing. After that, it was thought that I'd passed the critical stage, where things could go wrong if I'd kept moving and twisting. The bone was still a little bit tender, but I was allowed to start soft sand running. I went back to my pre-season fitness training of getting up at 5.30 in the morning and going for runs and a few sprints along Balmoral beach. My back started feeling better each day, but I was still very cautious. Basically I had to reload the bone again, and continue with a very measured comeback that would hopefully start with a few short spells during the one-day series against the West Indies and Zimbabwe. But the focus was the Indian trip.

I had more scans in early January just before the first of the one-dayers. The results showed there was brand new bone forming over the stress line, which made the doctors think that it had been a brand new injury. It was at that stage that I was very grateful to Errol Alcott for originally suggesting a scan because if I'd continued bowling I could have been out of cricket for

12 months. No India, no Ashes, and a frustrating winter at home concentrating on Australia's next home summer. I'd been very lucky.

I returned to bowling two days before the one-day series began when I had five overs at the MCG nets. I pulled up really well, but it was thought it would be too soon for me to come back into the team for the first game against the West Indies. So, it was decided I'd play the second match against them in Brisbane.

I rang up Dennis Lillee for a bit of reassurance. He stressed that I had to make sure my action was fluent and straight because there was a time in the Perth Test when I was getting a little side on again and mixing up the position of my front arm.

On the day of the game I was so excited about being back that it felt as though I was making my debut for Australia all over again. It was written in the press that I was like a kid outside a candy store waiting for the doors to open, and there's no doubt that summed me up. I was back in the green and gold, I had the boots on, and I thought, 'What a great game cricket is. I'm back. This is fantastic.'

We bowled first, and I shared the new ball with Pidgey. I felt good in my opening spell. It was very hot and I found it hard to get my breath, but my general fitness felt good. I was also happy with my action, and there was no pain at all in my back.

But in my second spell, I felt a twinge again. This time it was lower down than the spot I'd injured in Perth. I kept bowling, but didn't enjoy it at all because I couldn't give my best, and as a result I felt I was letting the team down. I couldn't even bring out my trademark leap when I had Jimmy Adams caught by Damien Martyn down at fine-leg. It was my only wicket, and although we ended up winning the match easily I was really concerned about my back. After doing some pressing around the spot, Errol Alcott seemed to think it was a muscular problem. Luckily it was, but I still had to rest for our next game as a precaution.

But it all came crashing down in Perth. It was only my fourth game of the series, and I was yet to get my rhythm back. I'd gone for 1–70 off 8 overs against Zimbabwe in Melbourne a couple of games earlier, and was keen to get some consistency back. It was hard to expect too much too quickly after coming back from such a long lay-off. I thought the pace was basically there, but I just didn't have the rhythm.

I made a similar start at the WACA against Zimbabwe, and got hit for some boundaries early on. All it takes is one or two balls to go through the field, then all of a sudden you're going for 12 to 14 runs an over. Sometimes these things happen, but I wasn't that worried because I was still easing myself back.

Then it all went really wrong. I was fielding at fine-leg, and Ricky Ponting was at deep mid-wicket. A ball was clipped out our way, and at first I thought it was going to split us and go for four. I was going to run around and try to dive, but I saw Punter screaming across so I stood back and let him have a go. He did a massive dive right in front of me, stopped the ball, and flicked it back to me all in the one motion. I was throwing into a breeze, so I tried to ping the ball really flat and hard to Gilly. As soon as I let it go I felt this big bang, this big snap in my arm. There was instant pain as my arm dropped down. It was limp by my side, and was buzzing with pins and needles. It felt as though the whole arm had separated at the elbow.

But I stayed out there. The next ball I threw in, I couldn't get any power at all, but the pain was still there. At that stage Tugga had asked me to warm up for my second spell, and I didn't want to let him down by saying I was hurt. I tried to bowl but my pace was right down. Tugga immediately wondered if my back was OK. It always takes me a while to warm up in my second spell, but the whole of that first over was slow.

The next over was no better. And in the third, a ball was hit past me towards mid-on. I chased it, did a slide and threw it back to Gilly's end with a side arm action. It killed me! As I was walking back to my mark I was in such incredible pain that I had to stop and pretend my shoelaces needed doing up until my arm stopped hurting so much. I had tears in my eyes. There were so many questions going through my mind. Should I go off and get myself right for the finals? Or did I keep bowling? And if I did keep bowling, would I hurt the arm even more? What about India and the Ashes? Was I in doubt? What were the boys thinking? Did they know I was injured? The last thing I was thinking about was where I should be bowling which, of course, should have been the only thing on my mind.

I was bowling only with my shoulder. I was trying not to use the wrist or arm at all. It didn't hurt as much as when I threw, but there was still significant pain there. At the end of the over I knew I had no choice. I walked over to Tugga and said, 'My arm is cooked. I think I've thrown it out. I think I might have broken it.' Tugga told me to go off and show it to Errol Alcott straight away.

Errol felt the arm, and when he pulled it gently it felt as though the whole bone was pulling apart. He told me he thought I had torn my medial ligament, and there could have been bone damage as well. I was sent to hospital for X-rays and the doctor came back with the results, unable to believe that I had bowled for three overs with the injury. My ulna bone was broken, and the medial ligament had been stripped from the bone. The doctor said it was the first time he'd seen an arm snap from throwing a ball. He'd seen ligament damage, but nothing as severe as mine. It showed there must have been an amazing amount of stress and force put on the arm.

As soon as I heard the word 'broken' I thought, 'Oh shit. How long does that mean now?' Errol said I could say goodbye to India, and the chances of the Ashes were also extremely doubtful. I was put on the red-eye flight to Melbourne that night to be examined by Australia's team doctor, Trefor James, first thing in the morning. It was the worst flight I'd ever been on because my arm was throbbing in a sling, and although I was a bit high on painkillers nothing could take the discomfort away.

When Trefor examined the arm, the news didn't get any better. I had to be booked in for an operation with surgeon Greg Hoy. At best, it looked as though I'd be out for three months. At worst, it was six months or longer. I was shattered. I'd worked hard on overcoming my back injury, and now this. At first I thought I was being cursed, and I went through a stage of thinking, 'What if Punter hadn't fielded the ball? What if he'd thrown it in himself? What if the wind wasn't against me? What if I'd stopped the ball and flicked it back to Punter?' But then there comes a time with every injury where you start to think that you can't feel sorry for yourself, and you just have to accept what has happened. I'm a firm believer in saying 'things happen for a reason'. Maybe the arm injury was my body's strange way of telling me my back hadn't healed properly, and I needed more time to rest. Who knows. I tried to remain positive, cop it on the chin, and get on with the recovery.

The operation went really well. I had two screws inserted in the ulna, and a piece of bone was grafted from my hip to further strengthen the area. The ligament was also anchored back onto the bone. The arm was so sore on the first day after the operation that I was put on morphine. It really knocked me about. I couldn't eat for two to three days, and then when I did start to have some food again I'd end up throwing everything up. Looking at my arm didn't help my state of mind. It was so swollen that I couldn't even see one knuckle in my hand. But slowly I began to recover and the pain started to ease. I spent five days in a plaster cast, then three weeks in a special 'Robocop' brace. Then the rehabilitation began. At an examination in early March, a month after the injury happened, Greg Hoy was really pleased with my progress and it was thought I'd be back bowling within a month. I was back on track for the Ashes in July and, although I knew I had to be very careful, I was jumping out of my skin to be ready for England.

Brett's race to be fit was closely monitored by Australia's medical staff, and also Steve Waugh, who was keen to have his fastest bowler back. Brett's absence from the Indian tour was significant. Australia lost 2–1 in what turned out to be one of the most remarkable Test series in history. Jason Gillespie and Glenn McGrath took 25 wickets between them to carry the Australian attack, but with spinners Shane Warne and Colin Miller proving ineffective, Waugh was left to rue the freakish accident that had sidelined Brett. The Australians needed their speedster for the Ashes against an English team growing in confidence following series wins in Pakistan and Sri Lanka. The race against the clock was on.

★   ★   ★

There was a strange twist of fate the day Brett broke his arm in Perth. Hours earlier on the other side of the country Shane walked out to bat at North Sydney Oval in a Mercantile Mutual Cup match against Western Australia. The Blues were struggling at 2 for 24 after losing Michael Slater and Brad Haddin. It could have been worse when Shane thrust forward defensively to the first delivery he received — a Jo Angel leg cutter. There was a noticeable sound, prompting Angel to lead his team into celebration after the ball thudded into the gloves of wicket-keeper Ryan Campbell. However, the Warriors' hi-fives quickly turned to hands on hips and glares of disbelief when the appeal was rejected.

Shane was adamant he hadn't edged the ball. Unaffected by the incident, he carried on to record his highest score of the summer — 115, including five sixes, off 126 deliveries. The innings helped sweep the Blues to an imposing 8 for 302, and an eventual 60 run victory. Shane recalls:

That innings was at the tail-end of one of the hardest times of my cricket career. A month earlier I'd missed out on the Australian team for the one-dayers. At the time we were midway through a Pura Cup game against South Australia in Adelaide. David Sincock, the NSW manager, read the team out during a tea break, and when my name was missing I immediately thought 'Stuff it. What have I done wrong?'

I couldn't think that last session when we went back out onto the field. As captain I was trying to be upbeat for the team, but it was so hard, almost impossible. I found it so hard to talk. I was shattered. I was just starting to build some momentum, and had enjoyed a great time the previous Australian season. I'd also done pretty well during the indoor series against South Africa, and believed I was the best bowler during the ICC tournament in Kenya. I don't think I had a right to be picked, but I'd really been looking forward to the summer. I looked at the 2000–01 season as a chance to cement my Australian spot. I knew my form hadn't been that great in the Pura Cup, but I still thought I'd get in.

I found it really hard for the next few games, and my performances were terrible. I thought I'd copped some bad luck and I began asking myself: 'How long is this going to continue?' It was bloody tough. I'd been in and out of the side before, but this time it seemed much worse. It was hard for me to watch any of the games on TV, and I really missed being with Brett. But after a couple of weeks, I realised it was no use moping around and worrying about it. I had to turn my attitude around, so I went back to sticking to the old cliché of taking things one ball at a time. That might sound simple, but it's so true. You can't do anything about what is in the past, and you can't do anything about what is in the future. So, you just have to make sure you get the present right.

The game against WA helped change my fortunes, and also gave the team some fresh confidence. We'd come off a hiding two weeks earlier in Perth after Murray Goodwin had smashed 167 against us, so it was good to reverse the roles at North Sydney. I was really happy with my innings. I picked the ball up quickly, and felt confident from very early on. It was a huge relief. Australia's chairman of selectors Trevor Hohns saw the innings, and said next day in the papers that the selectors were waiting to see more innings like that from me. At least I knew what I had to do.

That match was also one of the funniest I'd played in because of Don Nash's innings — 61 not out off 28 balls. Unbelievable! It was the second fastest fifty in Australian domestic limited overs history. He was smashing sixes everywhere (six in all), and all we could do in the dressing room was laugh. Nashy is not your typical-looking sportsman. He's a big bloke who likes a good feed. The night before the match he'd had calamari for dinner. And when we were hit with a random drug test after the match, we were all joking that Nashy would only be able to pass ink!

We really gained momentum because of that match. Our form in the one dayers had been pretty good all the way through, and after beating the WACAS we knew we could win the whole competition. They finished on top of the table, and we came second after beating Tasmania in the final round. So, we went back to Perth for the final. Although we hadn't won a trophy for seven years, Steve Rixon and I stressed to the team that we were under no pressure. We were a young and pretty inexperienced side when compared with the Warriors, who were also playing on added emotion because it was going to be Tom Moody's last one-dayer in Australia. Tom deserved to go out a winner, but not against us.

Moody gained a minor victory by winning the toss and deciding to bat on a pitch that promised to be full of runs. And so it proved. Despite slumping to 7 for 185, the Warriors recovered to reach 7 for 272 at the end of their 50 overs. Mike Hussey — 84 not out off 68 balls — was the saviour after sharing an unbroken 87 run stand with Kade Harvey.

However, Hussey's innings was overshadowed by Michael Bevan, whose unbeaten 135 off 137 balls was the glowing difference between the teams. Fittingly, the world's most consistent limited overs batsman hit the winning runs with ten balls and six wickets to spare. Shane made only 6, but there were no signs of disappointment in the beer-soaked dressing room afterwards.

The victory was the highlight of Shane's domestic season. His young outfit had defied the more experienced sides in the competition to give NSW its sixth limited overs title. In his eleven matches Shane had scored 289 runs at an average of 36.12, and a strike rate of 87.04. He also took eight wickets.

A week after the final, NSW carried its form into the Pura Cup with an emphatic 8 wicket win in Sydney over eventual champions, Queensland. Shane (114), Bevan (111), and young left hander Mark Higgs (181 not out) dominated the Blues' first innings total of 499. Another talented left hander, Nathan Bracken, then did the damage with the ball, taking 4 for 44 as the Bulls folded for 276 and were forced to follow on. In his best all-round game of the season, Shane gained considerable reverse swing in the second innings, capturing 3 for 10 off just four overs. Queensland was dismissed for 247, leaving NSW 25 for victory:

That game was our best team win for the season, but not my most memorable win. I don't think I'll ever forget my first Pura Cup match as captain after Steve Waugh and the other Test guys went away. It was against Western Australia again at North Sydney Oval. I don't reckon the WACAS like that ground much. We were 187 behind on the first innings and ended up setting the Warriors only 141 to win. The WA guys were pretty cocky and we'd been copping a bit of stick from them, but Nathan Bracken shut them up. He took five wickets, the Warriors were rolled for 89, and we'd won by 51 runs. It was fantastic, one of the best wins I've ever been associated with at any level. That's what makes cricket such a great game. You just never know what to expect.

I think NSW can be pretty happy with its performances for the season. We finished fourth in the Pura Cup, and considering one match against South Australia was a wash-out we could have finished higher. My batting and bowling form was up and down (365 runs at 33.18, and 17 wickets at 27.23), but I was satisfied that I'd played a significant role as captain. It was great to have Steve Waugh there for the first few games of the season. When you have the chance to be with players like Steve, you don't have to ask questions to learn new things. All you have to do is watch, and take in as much as you can. The field placings, the bowling changes, slowing the game down, speeding it up. A captain has to be his own man, but I know both Steve and Mark Taylor have influenced the way I think.

Looking back, the season was a real mix of highs and lows. Obviously my dumping from the Australian team was the worst moment, but I knew I'd get another chance. And it was up to me to make the most of that chance when it came. But I certainly didn't expect it to come as soon as it did. The season was over, the Aussies were in India for a one-day series before the Tests, and it was time for me to let off a bit of steam. One Friday after leaving work in North Sydney I settled in for a few drinks with Neil Maxwell at Blueberries, a local bar. The next thing you know I was getting home in pretty rough shape early Saturday morning. I was looking forward to a good sleep, but a couple of hours later the phone rings and I'm told I have to get my gear packed and get on a 4 o'clock flight to India because the team is struggling with injuries. I just panicked. I couldn't find anything, but somehow I got to the plane on time, and three days later I was playing in the fourth match of the series at Visakhapatnam. It was a bloody hot day. We batted first on an absolute belter. Bevo and I put on 34 in the last two and half overs to take us to 4 for 338. I got 25 off 11 balls. I was timing everything, but to be honest by that stage of the innings the Indians looked pretty ragged.

I suppose I'll remember that match mostly for bowling only three overs before suffering some sort of heat stroke or virus. It had hit me by the second over, and I was just stuffed! My face went beetroot red, and I just felt as if a truck had slammed into me. It was pretty embarrassing to go off in front of the boys — they gave me a bit of a hard time — but India can do that to you. One minute you're OK, then the next minute you're down for the count. We ended up winning the game, and a week later I was back in Australia. It was quite a bizarre experience, but that's the life of the modern day sportsman. You have to be prepared all the time because you just never know when you're going to get a call up to the big time. I know I'll get more chances in the future. The whole Australian team has improved since I first played. I'm looking forward to the future. I want to be part of it. And I know I can be.

CHAPTER SEVENTEEN

ASHES AND ACES

'Get better soon mate. The team misses ya.'
An old jogger passing by Brett during an early morning run at
Sydney's Balmoral Beach, March 2001.

The picturesque Balmoral Beach, in Sydney's northern suburbs, is a hive of activity nearly every morning of the year. As soon as sunlight begins tickling the yawning stretches of sand, hundreds of people from all avenues of life, begin stretching, swimming, running, walking dogs, and doing anything else that helps kick-start their days. Afterwards at sidewalk cafes, newspapers are read, cappuccinos are sipped, and muesli is crunched. It was in this vibrant setting that Brett began his race against time. A month after the surgery on his arm, he had resumed fitness training — a routine that usually began with six o'clock runs at Balmoral. Two months after surgery, he was back bowling off a few paces under the close scrutiny of NSW physiotherapist Pat Farhart.

Brett recalls:

I always knew I'd be back sooner rather than later because I was pretty used to judging how my body recovered from injuries. And it didn't take long after surgery for me to be feeling pretty good about my arm. It was getting stronger day by day, but the final decision would be left to Trefor James and Greg Hoy. I had a final examination in Melbourne in mid-May, just a couple of weeks before the Australian team would leave for the one-dayers against England and Pakistan. Luckily the X-rays showed everything was OK. The bone had healed properly and the screws had taken place. I was given the all clear, but was told I had to continue working back slowly to full pace before putting too much stress on the arm. At that stage I thought I'd be fit enough to play in the later games of the one-day series in early June, but it was much more important to take it easy and make sure I was ready for the Test series that started in July.

I joined up with the squad a week after they'd arrived in England. It was planned that I'd continue my way back by bowling limited spells at training. Then all of a sudden I went from bowling off limited run-ups in the nets to marking out my full length run-up in our first match of the one-day series against Pakistan in Cardiff. It all happened so fast. The morning of the match Jason Gillespie walked past me in the team hotel and said: 'You'd better be ready to play today Binga because I'm not looking that flash.' Dizzy was struggling with his hamstring, and Damien Fleming and Nathan Bracken were already out with injuries. The next thing I knew, Steve Waugh was sitting next to me on the team bus on the way to the ground. He asked me if I had any one-day gear with me, but I didn't because I wasn't actually in the original squad. Our manager Steve Bernard quickly sorted out a shirt, and Warney came to the party with a pair of pants. Steve Bernard handled all the official duties that enabled me to be added to the squad, and with next to no notice I was back in Aussie colours.

It was all a bit of a shock. My first spell in a match in England was going to be in an international! Tugga told me just to ease back into it. It was a strange feeling because I even had to remember how many steps I had to take for my run-up again; it had been such a long time since I'd been off the full run. Tugga was great and very reassuring. He said: 'Take your time. Don't worry about your pace. Just get your line and length right.'

I started OK, and actually thought I was going better than I'd planned. But I copped some stick in the final overs and ended up with 1–85 off 10. It was an Australian record. Not very pretty, but I wasn't expecting too much. It was just good to be back. And it was even better because we'd started with a win. I felt better as the series went along, and it was good to play an important part in our victory in the final at Lord's against Pakistan. I took 2–20, and felt reasonably happy with my progress.

Unfortunately much of the talk after the match was about the crowd behaviour during the trophy presentation. We'd been standing on the balcony clapping the Pakistan team when Michael Bevan copped a full can of beer flush in the face from someone below us. I was standing right next to Bevo. He bent over and started asking me if I could see any blood. I was so glad that he was OK because it would have taken only another couple of centimetres for the can to have hit Bevo in the eye. And that could have caused enough damage to wreck his career. It was an ugly incident, but not our only one for the series. In an earlier game against Pakistan at Trent Bridge, I was at the centre of Tugga's decision to lead the team off the field. I'd been fielding down at fine leg when a boy in the crowd was hit by a fire-cracker. The poor kid had to be treated by the paramedics, and that made me aware that I wasn't in the safest of places. A couple of overs later there was a huge 'crack' just a couple of feet away from me. A cracker had gone off right next to me. It scared the hell out of me. Bevo had also been having a bad time on the boundary, so I went to Tugga and told him there was no way I wanted to field close to the crowd. I told him my ears were ringing, and I was worried for my safety. He agreed straight away, and didn't muck about. He said: 'Binga, I've told the officials before I won't cop this. Mate we're going off. Playing cricket like this isn't worth it.' So Tugga told the umpires, then off we went. He was pretty angry. Luckily the incident was sorted out, and we went back out to finish the match, but it made all of us aware just how much danger players in any sport can be in. I hope it never happens, but there is always a chance that some day a player will end up seriously hurt because of an idiot in the crowd.

Off the field, I had the chance to face another type of missile. In the lead up to Wimbledon, a promotional event was arranged between me and the world's fastest server Greg Rusedski, who had a record serve of 149 miles per hour. Greg got kitted up in the Australian gear and faced a few of my deliveries. I didn't bowl too quickly, but fast enough to make him hurry a bit. He kept trying to hit me with bottom hand top-spin slogs. You could tell he was a tennis player. Then it came my turn on the court. Greg told me he'd start by serving a couple of balls down the line. I didn't even see the first few! I'd been used to playing against Shane, who was a really hard server, but nothing like this guy. He was spitting out rockets! Obviously it was very different to facing a cricket ball because the angle was really different, and the amount of spin on the ball made it almost impossible for me to judge anything. After a while I managed to pick a few up, but I still found it really hard to get a racquet on them. Greg said he was serving at about 130 miles an hour. No wonder these guys have a lot of shoulder problems. It was a terrific experience, and gave me a greater appreciation of other professional sportsmen. I'll never watch a tennis match in the same way again.

The promotion was a really quick break for me before the Test series began. After the one-day final we only had two games before the First Test at Edgbaston. I didn't play the first match against the MCC, but came in for the second against Essex at Chelmsford. It turned out to be one of my most enjoyable moments of the tour. Or at least with the bat anyway. The match was heading for a draw by the second innings, so a few of the guys were keen for some time in the middle. Part of our innings also coincided with a State of Origin Rugby League match between NSW and QLD that was being shown live on television. When we were one wicket down, Mark Waugh was supposed to be the next bloke in, but he said: 'Binga, you can go in next. I want to watch the Origin, so don't get out for eighty minutes'! Sure enough a wicket fell, and I was on my way to the middle filling in for Junior. I was lucky. Once I got through the first half hour, I felt OK, and started to get a few runs. I passed 30, 40, 50, then by the time I got to 60 I started thinking: 'Geez Binga, you're a chance for 100 here!' That's when I got into trouble because I started thinking like a batsman! I ended up being stumped for 79 off Peter Such. I'd gassed it!

There was a huge buzz in the camp leading up to the First Test. We were all really excited and pumped. As a boy, I'd always dreamt of playing in the Ashes. It was the ultimate. So I couldn't stop thinking about it in the days leading up to Edgbaston. I had good chats to some of the senior guys in the team, especially Glenn McGrath. He just told me to enjoy it, and make the most of the opportunities I'd be given.

We were expecting it to be a really hard game. England might have lost their last Test to Pakistan at the start of the season, but they still had every right to be confident after their recent successes on the subcontinent. And with a home crowd behind them, they were sure to be pretty fired up. The media were really expecting big things from them, but it didn't take long for everything to be put in perspective. Tugga sent England in, Warney cleaned them up with 'five-for', then Tugga, Damien Martyn and Gilly all clicked with centuries, and before you knew it, we had a 282 run lead on the first innings.

My contributions were pretty forgettable. I took 0–71 off 12 overs, and got cleaned up for a golden duck after I edged a ball to Mike Atherton off Mark Butcher. But it didn't matter because we were in a match-winning position.

England's second innings surprised me. They were rolled for 164. Their effort showed up one of the big differences between the teams. Once we had got on top, England became very negative. They began playing as though they expected to lose. They wouldn't back themselves at all. The contrast between the captains was huge. Tugga was always so confident and aggressive, but Nasser Hussain was nowhere near as assured. It summed up his Test when Dizzy broke his finger in the second innings to put him out for the next two Tests. Dizzy and Warney both took three wickets. We ended up winning by an innings and 118 runs. I took 2–37. I'll always remember my first Ashes wicket — a short ball from around the wicket that Mark Butcher nicked through to Gilly. It was a great relief to get that wicket. I was hoping it would have come sooner than it did, but bowling in England was a whole new experience. It was my first time; the wickets were slower, and the grounds were a lot smaller. I had to learn to bowl a fuller line and length. There was no doubt that the English balls swung around a lot more than in Australia, so I had to try to make the most of that. Bowling first change was also going to be a challenge because I'd always taken the new ball all the way through grade and into first-class cricket. Admittedly it was difficult to adjust, but Pidgey and Dizzy were two world-class bowlers, and if that meant I'd have to bowl more regularly at first change, then I was happy with that. I was still playing for Australia.

My learning curve continued in the Second Test at Lord's. We won easily again by eight wickets. Junior scored a century, and it was Pidgey's turn to take the bowling honours with 8 scalps for the match. I can never get tired of watching him bowl because his control is just so great and his ability to think batsmen out is the best in the world. He is a great.

I took a wicket in each innings, and copped a bit of a serve in the media for the run-ins I had with Mike Atherton and Graham Thorpe in the second innings. When I came on to bowl, Tugga asked me to crank it up against Atherton. Early on I pitched one short, which Atherton pulled away for four. That got me a little pumped up, so I really tried to bend my back. I started to let a few short ones go, and that created a bit of a buzz around the crowd. Then Thorpe started egging me on when he was facing. He was saying things like: 'That ball was slow mate. That the best you can do?' I'd hit back with: 'Well we'll wait to see where the next one goes.' We exchanged a few words, and there was a little bit of conflict, but it was just the emotion of Test cricket showing out. I couldn't see a problem with it. It would have been better for my bowling to do all of the talking, but I don't think I overstepped the line. It was just a spur of the moment reaction. I had the last say when I broke one of his fingers, then trapped him lbw for 2. It was great to see him walking off after having our 'chat'. I suppose I won that battle; the psychology came off. The whole build-up made it the most satisfying of my wickets in the series up until that time.

Playing at Lord's was one of the greatest moments I'd had. It was the one Test I was keen to play in more than any other. The whole atmosphere made it a magical experience. The carpet-like grass, the old member's grandstand, the long room, the members in their ties and straw hats. I wanted to soak up everything. It was a very special feeling, and actually took a while to get used to because at first I imagined how many legends of the game had played their before me. How many had walked through the long room. How many had walked down the steps and received pats on the back from the members. How many cricketers had done their boots up on the seats. Cricketers like Bradman. It gave me tingles thinking I was actually in some very small way a member of the same club. I was becoming part of history. And history is such a big thing at Lord's. I just wanted to take it all in, and enjoy every moment as something few people are lucky enough to experience . . . a privilege.

We also met the Queen during the tea interval on the first day. That was great. We lined up in single file, and Tugga led her along the line. When she got to me she asked if it was my first time in England, and whether I was enjoying it. I didn't really know what to say. I was a bit overwhelmed. I stumbled over a few words saying that I was having a great time, then she smiled and moved on. After the formalities she came over to a group of us and just started talking more casually. She even apologised for the weather being so bad in London because we'd had a few days of rain. It was fantastic to meet her; she seemed a very humble person. There are so many thousands of people who'd love to meet high-profile people like the Queen, but never get the chance. It makes me realise just what a privileged position I am in. Playing at Lord's and meeting the Queen were two of the biggest highlights of the trip.

The biggest highlight undoubtedly came in the Third Test at Trent Bridge when we retained the Ashes. The game was the toughest one we'd had to that stage of the tour. England struggled to 185 after Atherton won the toss and batted first. Pidgey was again the main man with 5–49. I bowled Andy Caddick to finish off the innings, and although I'd only bowled seven overs, I felt for the first time in the series that I was beginning to get back into a rhythm. We'd aimed to get England out for under 200, so we thought we were in a really good position when we started our innings, but we collapsed to 7–102. To fight back from there was our first true test of the series. We really had to buckle down. It was great for us because it knocked any complacency out of the team. It suddenly became much more of a challenge than the first two Tests. Thanks to Gilly's half-century we got a five run lead, then Warney took 6–33 to roll England for 162. I took Mark Butcher's wicket, and continued feeling a lot more comfortable with the way the ball was coming out.

We lost 3 wickets and our captain while knocking off the 158 runs to win. Tugga was carried off with a torn calf muscle after going for a single from the first ball he'd faced. It was a sickening sight from the dressing room. Tugga never shows pain unless he's in really big trouble. It was upsetting to see him in such a bad way. It also put some pressure on the team. We'd lost a couple of quick wickets, then all of a sudden Tugga was going off on a stretcher. He was rushed away to have the injury assessed, but John Buchanan stressed that we had to continue focusing on the cricket, and thankfully we got home with a good partnership between Marto and Junior. The fact that the winning run came from an Andy Caddick no-ball summed up England's campaign.

When we needed about 10 runs to win, the team started gathering on the balcony, and when Caddick bowled the no-ball, the whole team went up as one. It was the best feeling ever to know we'd won the Ashes. It was magical. I remember Ricky Ponting putting his arm around me and yelling: 'How good is this Binga!'

By the time all the presentations had been done, it was still early afternoon, but we stayed in the change room until late that night. I was really happy that Mum and Dad were at the ground. They came up with a number of the players' wives and girlfriends to join in the party. We were just one big family. I'll never forget it. At 11.30 we were still waiting for Punter to lead the team song. Everyone was beginning to wonder when he'd do it. Then all of a sudden he broke into it: 'Underneath the Southern Cross I stand . . .' I don't think I'd ever shouted it with such passion. We'd been waiting hours and hours — for me it was really a lifetime — so every word meant everything to me. How could I ever want to be doing anything else? At that stage I looked around me and thought I was the luckiest guy in the world.

CHAPTER EIGHTEEN

STROBES AND STRUMS

*The band is just a fun thing. It's no different to
going out and playing golf. We're not going out
to whack a white ball over 18 holes, instead we go
into a studio and play music for three hours for a bit of
fun. When we play a gig, people set up everything for
us, and we just turn up and play. It's like we're just
going out to have dinner or go to the pictures, and
that's the way we treat it.*

Gavin Robertson, 'Riddler',
off-spinner and drummer, Six and Out

Nearly every backyard cricket player knows the feeling of sweetly striking a full toss over the geraniums into the next door neighbour's yard to the gleeful yell of the bowler, 'You're gone. That's six and out.'

The expression 'six and out' is as Australian as barbeques and blowflies. And now, it also conjures images of Riddler, Buzzard, Cheeks, Binga, and Shane-O strumming, sweating, and singing their way through a set at the Coogee Bay or the Ettamogah Pub on a Friday night.

The first steps towards rock stardom — a term that the band members insist be used very loosely — were taken in the NSW dressing room during the 1996–97 season. Off-spinner Gavin Robertson, all-rounder Brad McNamara, and Shane were sitting having a chat over beers after a match. The conversation soon swung from cricket to music. Gavin had the strongest musical background: his mother was a dancer in the 1950s and '60s, travelling much of country New South Wales on bandstand tours. When not at cricket or soccer training as a boy, Gavin recalls he was often dancing and singing with his sister and mother in the back room of their home in Sydney's western suburbs:

It was great fun, but by the time I was 13 I thought I was a bit too cool for dancing, so I started playing drums. Who was to know I was going to combine cricket with music all these years later. During our chat in the dressing room, Buzzard said he wanted to learn the guitar. Shane had already started. So, I suppose you could say the first seeds were sown then.

McNamara had no musical experience, but he'd always wanted to learn the guitar and was encouraged by Shane. McNamara says:

Shane had taken it up a few years earlier. He kept telling me it was great fun, so I eventually thought, 'Bugger it. I'll give it a crack.' So I went and bought an old acoustic, Shane taught me a few of the basics, and I took it from there. It's bloody hard work when you teach yourself. You get to a real sticking point for the first two or three months, fingers go everywhere, but you've just gotta push through it. I actually thought I was never going to be able to do it, but you just have to keep persisting and slowly you notice the change.

Shane too had taught himself, but he had an advantage because he had a musical background. He and his brothers had dabbled with piano lessons as boys, but Grant was the only one to take to it with enthusiasm. These days, the youngest Lee is an accomplished keyboard player who can turn his hand to most instruments with enviable ease. Bob Lee says:

I'll tell you how much music means to Grant. When Shane was old enough to drive, I said I would help him buy a second-hand car. He came back one day and said he'd found the one he wanted. It was a very old black BMW. I went and had a look at it with him and the doors had been resprayed and there were rust bubbles everywhere. I told him to take it back, and Helen and I'd help him buy a new car instead. We went halves with him in a new Barina. We did the same thing with Brett, and we gave Grant the choice of money towards a car or a piano. He chose the piano.

The musical wheels turned more slowly for the older Lee boys. Shane first dabbled with the guitar in 1995 when he was inspired by 'More than Words', a song by the band Extreme. He bought a teaching-aid CD and a book of chords and started playing whenever he could, including on tours. However, it wasn't until after the dressing-room chat with Robertson and McNamara that the thoughts of a band slowly gained momentum. Shane and McNamara took guitars to England during the '97 winter to pass the time when they weren't playing league cricket. On their return, they joined Robertson for a few light-hearted studio sessions. By this time Brett had caught the bug:

There was no bass player, and when I came onto the scene for Shield cricket I remember sitting around while these guys were having a jam session, and I thought, 'Well I'm not going to get into this band as a singer, so I better teach myself how to play the guitar.' So I went out with Grant, who knew more about music than all of us put together. I was going to buy an acoustic at first, but Grant persuaded me to get a bass, and next day I rocked up to cricket training and said, 'Boys, I've got a bass, and I'm gonna join the band. I'm in!' I went home, Grant started teaching me a few things, and before you know it I was hooked. I loved it. Playing the bass is a bit like fast bowling. It gets me pumping. I get it, slap it, and hit it really hard. It's unreal. That suits me down to the ground.

Brett joined the group in 1998, but the band was still without a name and, more importantly, a lead singer. Enter Richard Chee Quee:

In '97 I was also playing English league cricket in Bolton, only 15 minutes away from Buzzard and Shane. We used to get together for a few sessions, and I'd do a bit of the singing. The love for it all went back to when I was a kid. Mum was born and raised in Fiji, and music was part of her culture. I actually grew up with sing-alongs and the drinking of kava in our Sydney backyard. I used to love sitting and listening to Mum and all the family's Fijian and Samoan friends get together. I guess my harmony came from that. If I have any!

But the playing of instruments had never been a big thing in the family. We got a piano when I was pretty young, but it was more of an ornament than anything. It was just to make the dining room look pretty good. I sort of mucked around with it and picked up a few tunes by ear here and there.

I was also in a brass band at school. I played the double B flat bass, the big tuba. Imagine that! I didn't really want to, but I joined the band to get out of some of the other classes.

When I started playing cricket for NSW, we were always mucking around with music at training or in the dressing rooms. Music becomes a big part of a cricketer's life because it can help you relax when you're on the road a lot. When the chance came to give singing a go with the others, I thought it was going to be a lot of fun.

By mid-1998, the band had been officially formed. As Robertson recalls, the hard work was just beginning:

At first we learnt a bunch of about 12 cover songs, and we started to think, 'Wow, we can do this.' We played eight songs very poorly at the '98 NSW team Christmas party, but we all knew we could do something more. We had to pull together a bit tighter so we started rehearsing more, and the more rehearsals we did the tighter we got. We started to get quite good considering where we'd come from, but then we started to get real picky because something about us being cricketers made us perfection driven. We were trying too hard, and we got to the point where we said, 'Stuff it, let's just enjoy this and make this thing rock.' From then on we just had fun.

It was at that stage that the five would-be rockers tossed up names for their band, and decided they had to have a classic Australian colloquialism — but it must relate to cricket. They suggested: 'Full Tosses', 'No Ball', 'Caught Behind', 'Hit and Run', but nothing inspired them until 'Six and Out' was mentioned. It was as appropriate a name as any, although at some gigs the boys are occasionally asked by non-cricketing fans: 'Who's the sixth member of the band? Are you playing one short?'

The band attracted considerable public attention when they played at a testimonial fund-raising roast for Greg Matthews at Sydney's Regent Hotel in December 1998. They left the crowd of about 600 laughing, grinning, and shaking heads, as they belted out Australia's national anthem to the tune of the Proclaimers hit 'Five Hundred Miles'.

McNamara says:

That was our first really big public appearance. It was quite terrifying. To be honest, we were shitting ourselves. Because were were singing the national anthem, we were first up. And there were some pretty-big hitters in the room, like Kim Beazley. We were worried for two reasons: One, what happened if we upset people because we'd played around with the anthem? and, Two, what happened if we just sounded awful? Luckily we went OK.

There was obviously room for further improvement, but the signs were there that Six and Out wasn't going to be dismissed easily. And with the help of some of Australia's most well-known musicians — Tim and Andrew Farris (INXS), Dave Gleeson (Screaming Jets), John and Anthony Field (Cockroaches) and Greg Page (The Wiggles) — the cricketers-cum-musicians continued to improve. Among all the high-profile advisers, there was one person who became an integral part of the band's development: producer Garth Porter, who rose to stardom in the 1970s as a member of Sherbert, was invited by Brett and Shane's former manager, Peter Culbert, to meet the band at a training session during the 1998–99 season.

Sherbert, with lead singer Darryl Braithwaite, was one of the most popular bands of its time. And when on tour the members always packed a cricket kit to pass the hours offstage. One night, after returning from a gig in Wollongong, the idea of performing a cricket song bounced around the band's bus. Soon afterwards, Porter and bass player Tony Mitchell wrote 'Howzat', a song that would become one of Sherbert's signature pieces.

Twenty years later Porter was listening to a rough, and raw, rap version performed by Six and Out. Porter acknowledges:

I didn't need any persuading to meet the guys because I'm such a cricket nut. We got on really well, and one thing led to another. In September 1999 we did a three-track CD, including 'The Mighty Blues', a song about the NSW team. We mildly looked at a record deal then, but not that seriously because there weren't enough tracks to get our teeth into.

If they'd come to me as musicians, I think I would have said to them, 'Spend a bit more time honing your skills.' But they did have a different appeal because of who they were. I was at them right from the start to do some of their own songs. They were used to doing covers where you of course get a reaction from the crowds, but the music business is different to that. That is not a good look. The guys didn't think they could write, but we grabbed a guitar and went from there. They were never short of ideas, some were completely off the planet, but we kept at it. I encouraged them all to contribute as much as they could. We also sought help from Colin Buchanan, one of the most talented songwriters I know. Colin was rapt to be involved.

By June 2000 we were ready to record a full album, including five originals. By that stage I'd got to see them play live, and I knew what direction the CD should go. They were a pub rock band. I don't mean to belittle them at all, but there was no fancy pants sort of stuff. They were just the raw thing — plenty of guitars and rock and roll.

The studio sessions were a lot of fun, but hard work. One thing I really noticed was how well each of them handled criticism. When recording, you are exposed to pretty severe judgement where everything is under a magnifying glass; it's not like a hazy pub environment. They were good listeners, but were definitely their own biggest critics.

It was interesting watching them because they all had their own characteristics. Shane and Brett both had a great sense of timing. It might sound simple, but even the best musicians have problems with timing. The groove is everything in rock.

And their pitch? Well, listen to them sing. That was something right out of the box because at that stage neither of the boys were doing songs live, but I thought it would be really neat to see what they could do. So, one day at the studio I suggested Shane have a go at singing 'The Nips Are Getting Bigger'. Shane sat in the control room and mulled over it for a while. I reckon he was wondering if the NSW captain should be heard and seen singing such a song. There was also a little bit of trepidation because he was conscious of his own voice. But he decided to have a go. The first take was a bit rough around the edges, but I thought that was just a nerve thing. Then, the more he did it, the better and more surprising he was.

Binga went through the same kind of process. On his first attempt at vocals we did three takes, and tried again in a couple of days. The second attempt was just a quantum leap ahead of the first day. And then we did another two or three takes a few days after that, and the improvement was just as great again.

After about five hit outs at a song, both Brett and Shane started to express themselves really well. They were controlling their vocals, getting their timing together, and interpreting the songs well. They gave it their all, and they were really good.

Of the others, Riddler has a great instinct for the drums, and he has got a remarkably good voice. In the studio he was one of those funny guys that the more he thought about how difficult a problem was, the greater the problem became. But most of the time he just cut loose, and that's what I really liked. I didn't ask for anything too controlled.

They all improved incredibly from the first studio sessions we did in August 1999, and Buzzard was no exception. Sometimes he surprised me how well he did things. There were times when I thought, 'Buzzard is really going to struggle with this,' but he never did. Some of the things that I thought would be really tricky to do, Buzzard did them really quickly. Some of the things that I thought were really simple, we spent days on. He also proved to be a very talented lyric writer.

And Cheeks, well he can make songs his own. He really just put so much enthusiasm into them. I was a bit concerned at first because over-enthusiasm doesn't work on a record; it can sound too 'try hard', but Cheeks hit a real sweet spot where the energy was just right. He had good tone to his voice, a great attitude and excellent pitch. Plus he was a great showman.

The band invited some special guests to be part of the CD. Braithwaite tripped back in time to help sing 'Howzat', and Steve Waugh had a speaking part in 'Eleven', an original written by Porter and the band. As the first two verses and chorus suggest, the song reflected cricket through the ages:

Baggy Greens, Test in creams
SCG, childhood dreams
Bodyline, ninety-nine point nine
Windies tied, Hansie lied

McGilvray's call, underarm ball
McCosker's jaw, twins of Waugh
Healy stumps, blaster thumps
Lillee bumps, Howzat ump

It's the power of eleven
It's the spill of emotion
It's more than a game
A history aflame
It's the pride of a nation
Our spirits in motion
It's the roar of the crowd
Singin' out loud
Yeah, Whoa

Channel Nine adopted the chorus of 'Eleven' to promote Australia's 2000–01 international season involving the West Indies and Zimbabwe. Nine's personalities were well featured on the album. Sports commentator Ray Warren leant his distinctive tones to the cover version of Paul Kelly's hit 'Dumb Things', and Joe Previtera helped add a controversial touch by playing his role in the original 'Can't Bowl, Can't Throw'. Previtera, better known as 'Joe the Cameraman', was the man behind the infamous 'Can't bowl, can't throw' line that Shane Warne was initially suspected of uttering against Queensland paceman Scott Muller during the Second Test between Australia and Pakistan in Hobart in November 1999. A year later, just two weeks before the official launch of the album, Muller voiced his disapproval at the song's title in the media. But the boys from Six and Out said there was no hurt intended and, as its words indicated, the song wasn't about Scott at all:

I was trying out for the high-school cricket team
Dreamed one day I'd be wearin' that Baggy Green
I gave it all I got and when were done
The coach called me over and said, 'Sorry son'
But you can't bowl and you can't throw

I'm just telling you what everyone knows
Absolute sitters, you put down

All the tailenders hit you out of the ground
Don't ask Warney, it was Cameraman Joe
He'll say you —
Can't bowl and you can't throw

Went for an audition down at Channel Nine
Richie's job well, it was gonna be mine
They sent a message on the autocue
It said, 'Thanks for comin'
And —
We'll call you'

CHORUS

Well I met a good looker down at the local bar
And I told her she was talkin' to a big-time cricket star
Well I told her my stats and I dropped my name
She said, 'I've never heard of you, and I hate that game'

CHORUS

The self-titled CD was launched by ABC Music and EMI on 13 November 2000 in Sydney. Apart from 'Can't Bowl, Can't Throw' and 'Eleven' it includes the originals: 'Cyclone Sally', a song about a devoted fan; 'I've Been Dropped', which tells the story of a man out of luck from the cricket field and his experience in the workplace; and, despite its cricket connotations, 'It's Over', which paints a picture of a broken relationship. Porter, Colin Buchanan, Ben Hassell and renowned country performer Troy Cassar-Daly helped write the songs. The cover versions included are: 'The Nips Are Getting Bigger' (Mental as Anything), 'Just Keep Walking' (INXS), 'Howzat' (Sherbert), 'Psycho Killer' (Talking Heads), 'Eagle Rock' (Daddy Cool), and 'Dumb Things' (Paul Kelly).

The launch of the CD was the end of a project that took 12 weeks in the recording studio, twice as long as most albums Porter had produced. A video clip of 'Can't Bowl, Can't Throw' was released at the same time. Shot over two days, it was a comical portrayal of Brett as a hopeless cricketer, Shane as the future Richie Benaud of the commentary box, and Chee Quee as the luckless star who was rejected by a 'good looker' at the bar.

The band continued to play occasionally on the pub circuit after the launch, but regular gigs were hampered by cricket commitments. Shane says:

Obviously it will never replace cricket. It's just really good fun. It was nerve-racking at first, standing up in front of people. When I began playing I was concentrating so hard on playing the right notes at the right time that I sometimes got pretty stressed. But now, nights go really quickly. We just have to enjoy it, play up to the crowd, and make sure they enjoy it too. Most of the time the crowd doesn't expect us to be any good. After all, we're just a bunch of cricketers.

Music is a great release for us all. I wish I'd paid more attention to learning the piano when I was younger. I know when I become a parent, I'd love my kids to play an instrument.

Music has become an escape route for all band members, especially Brett and Shane, whose time away from cricket is invariably filled with sponsorship commitments and other duties connected to their on-field roles. Robertson says:

Being in the band has taught me a lot about Brett and Shane. It's an important release for both of them, but they still can't hide the people they are. When Brett is in the studio, he could be at the top of his mark bowling to Tendulkar. Everything is just total fun for him. He's the only guy in the band who dances around, and smiles at everything at rehearsals. He just loves it, he's a pig in mud. He has learnt the quickest of everyone.

There's no doubt Buzzard is technically the most advanced guitarist in the band, but Shane plays very good rhythm guitar. He works away, and doesn't like to stuff up. He likes to play to perfection. He can sing, but doesn't think he can. Brett loves to sing, and is getting better.

You know, they have some really good blues. There've been a few times when Brett has played the wrong chord and Shane will stop straight away and say, 'Binga, what the bloody hell are you doing?' Then, they'll have a massive argument over chords and Shane will ask, 'What are you doing mate? Are you concentrating or not? Are you with us?' And Brett will reply, 'Yeh, of course I am. I'm in the same room aren't I?' Binga is just so young about it all. Then they'll just shut up and do it again properly before they have a final exchange:

'That's it Binga.'

'I know.'

But I don't think I've ever come across two brothers who are as close as they are when it really counts. Once, during a trip to Melbourne for a gig, Brett had the flu really badly — to the point where he was shaking and vomiting. Shane just totally changed immediately. He was straight on the hotel phone and organising soup, a doctor and medication. He just went straight into big brother mode. There was no mucking around, there was no more laughter, and he was genuinely worried for a couple of hours. He sat next to Brett in bed and fed him soup every five minutes, and made sure everything was all right. You can't manufacture those times. The two of them joke around a bit, and they argue, but that moment when Brett was sick showed a really close bond. I felt privileged to be there. I know Shane will always look out for Brett, and it will work the other way as well, whether they're playing for Australia, or Six and Out.

CHAPTER NINETEEN

THE PRESENT AND FUTURE

*The first time I went out with Warney, we walked into a
pub and the place just stopped. You could hear and see
people saying, 'That's Shane Warne.' That opened my
eyes to the pressure some people can be under. Because
Warney is so much in the public spotlight, he is
scrutinised for whatever he does. But then again, that is
the role of the Test cricketer, and you've gotta learn to
deal with it. And how you deal with it is how you'll be
looked upon.*

Brett Lee

On the night of Neil Maxwell's buck's party in late 2000, a
rambling collection of cricketers, mates, and work colleagues
wandered their way through the pubs of Balmain and Sydney's
CBD. In the early hours of the morning at one particular
establishment, a middle-aged man, shirt out, and tie loosened after
a hard week of white-collar work, staggered his way towards Brett.
The man offered little introduction before thrusting a mobile
phone towards Brett's ear.

'It's my son,' the man said. 'Can you say hello to him.'

Without blinking or spilling a drop of his drink, Brett took the phone and spoke to the unknown voice at the other end of the line.

'Hello, it's good to talk to you,' he said with a smile. 'Do you play cricket?'

For the next few minutes Brett spoke to the boy, and wished him luck for the remainder of the season. He finished by saying, 'Make sure you have fun. That's the most important thing, mate.'

Brett gave the phone back to the man, shook his hand, smiled, then returned to his mates. It was just a typical moment during a night out on the town.

It's rarely possible for Brett or Shane to be out on a social occasion without beer coasters, business cards, toys, hats, handbags, even bare skin, being thrust in front of them with a pen and a hopeful smile close behind. Usually there are as many autographs signed, as many photos posed for, and as many hands shaken as there would be along the red carpet in Hollywood on Oscar night. Occasionally people consider their brush with stardom is the chance for one-upmanship. Like the time a drunk schoolboy rugby player asked Brett, 'Mate, aren't you that winger who plays for St George? I know I've seen your face somewhere. You're not real big for a footy player.'

But Brett and Shane have learnt to take the mixture of cheek and adulation in their stride. Such is Brett's popularity, a greyhound has even been named after him. It is simply part of life in the spotlight. Brett says:

There've been times when I've been out having a quiet drink with a mate and I've forgotten for a couple of hours that I play cricket, but then someone comes up and asks for an autograph. It makes me feel quite special. Of course there are times when I don't want to be disturbed, but when I have time to think about it, I know it is one of the duties that comes with the job. The majority of people who approach me are fantastic. They just want to have a bit of a chat, and I'm happy to talk to them. After all, I'd rather be in that position than not being wanted at all, because that means I wouldn't have achieved anything on the cricket field.

When it first started happening, I thought it would only last for a couple of weeks. But it hasn't stopped. I know in particular how important it is to be a role model to kids. It's a privilege to be given that responsibility. There's no better feeling than when a boy or girl comes up and asks me for an autograph. There might be some sportsmen who don't like signing because it's an invasion of personal space, but to me, you have to learn to love it. Quite often when I sign an autograph, I remember how excited I used to feel as a boy when I got a player's signature. Now, even if the line is long and it takes another 15 minutes to get every piece of paper signed, I know I have to do it. It's part of the game. It's strange how some people put us on pedestals. It's important when talking with kids to tell them that we are just the same as them — we are simply playing a game we love.

It's a big buzz. We really do have a huge responsibility both on and off the field because kids watch us so closely, especially on the television, and they copy everything we do. Whether it be rubbing the sweat off our eyes or the way we hold our bat, or what we say, we have to be very careful. But the responsibility is nothing we can't handle because it comes down to human nature, and how you've been brought up. Shane and I have a lot to thank Mum, Dad, and Grant for. They've given us love, support and guidance all the way.

Shane also acknowledges the role he has to play:

It shouldn't matter if it's a high-profile person, or the bloke down the street: if either of them do something wrong, then they should feel they've let themselves and others down. The only difference is that high-profile people are under much more scrutiny. Either way, everyone should know the difference between right and wrong.

Malcolm Speed made a very good point when Brett and I were doing our contract negotiations for 2000. Malcolm said if we were going to do something in public that we didn't want our family or girlfriends to read about, then we shouldn't do it. It's common sense. That not only goes for us, but everyone — whether you're in the public spotlight or not.

When it comes to public adulation, I'm very lucky because I have a nice balance. I can walk around Sydney and not get hassled. But it's different for Brett. I don't think he fully realises it yet. If he keeps climbing at the current rate, there'll come a time when he's going to struggle to even go out. There'll come a time when there'll be a picture of him walking out of a pub, or a shot of a girl grabbing him. And if it's taken the wrong way, then all of a sudden Brett's in trouble.

Thankfully, he's smart and has good people around him as well, from the family to his mates, and our manager Neil Maxwell. Lack of guidance, or poor guidance, gets a lot of professional sportspeople into trouble. Brett won't have that problem.

There was no better indication of Brett's popularity when he was named runner-up last April in *Cleo* magazine's annual Bachelor of the Year competition. But his public appeal spreads well beyond the pages of glossy magazines. Manager Neil Maxwell acknowledges Brett and Shane have become highly sought after commodities in the multimillion dollar world of sporting endorsements:

There's an X factor. I used to hear that jargon spoken all the time in marketing, but until you come across it you don't realise how powerful it is. It refers to those people who may have the looks, the moves, the mannerisms, anything that has that magnetic appeal to the public. There is something there that is an appealing factor about both the boys, especially Brett. Who knows what it is. But the fact that both have blond hair and good looks and are international sportsmen obviously has a lot to do with it. Throw in Six and Out, and Brett's tag as the world's fastest bowler, then it stands to reason there has to be enormous marketability there.

It's unbelievable how popular the boys are. I am new to the management game, and only took it up because of a close friendship with Shano and Brett. We simply shook hands on an agreement. I didn't know what to expect, and I admit I've been overwhelmed by their appeal in the marketplace.

Last year they appeared on Channel Nine's 'The Footy Show' in Sydney. Shane bowled an over of balls to Paul Harragon to raise funds for charity. The very next day, the phone rang hot with offers from various companies and charities. It was an amazing response.

But we have to be careful. Whatever happens in the future, there will always only be four to six main avenues of endorsements. Otherwise it's just not fair. We've had a lot of companies come knocking, many just looking for short-term fixes, but that just doesn't fit the boys' images.

One of the things that impresses me most about Shane and Brett is the very serious role Shane takes as the older brother. He looks after Brett to an extent that I find incredible, and he accepts Brett's potential fame and fortune really well. They have a very special relationship. The whole Lee family has a warmth to it. There is a lot of love between everyone, and it's pleasing to see such a humble family now reaping some rewards.

Despite the lucrative returns from endorsements, one of the most important names Brett and Shane have thrown their support behind is the New Day Foundation, a charity established by Sanitarium to aid the prevention of youth suicide. Brett donated his $5000 cheque from the *Cleo* Bachelor of the Year to the cause, one that is close to the hearts of the Lee family. Brett says:

Suicide is something Shane and I have both been touched by. Growing up we had a very close friend who we played cricket with. In 1999 he took his own life, leaving behind a girlfriend and two kids. No-one knew why it had happened, but he'd basically spoken to no-one about his problems. It was a very big shock to me; it really hit home. Shane and I had a chat, and we thought it would be a very worthwhile activity to get behind a charity we believed in. Through Sanitarium and Weet-Bix we started the New Day Foundation. There are hotlines for kids with problems, and a fun park has been established in Melbourne that allows troubled people to get away from their worries and talk to professional people. There's so much love at the park, and sensible guidance. We have to get the message across that not everything in a young person's life needs to be bad. Unfortunately there is so much negative press about society and the youth of today that it is easy to be dragged down with pessimism. Basically the target group is 15- to 24-year-olds. The cause has even greater significance for me and Shane because the Wollongong area has one of the highest suicide rates in Australia. That saddens me because when Shane, Grant and I were growing up we had everything you could dream of. Most of all we had a fantastic mum and dad. It makes me feel for everyone who hasn't been as fortunate, but the most important message is that no-one should give up hope because we all have so much to live for. Hopefully Shane and I can use our cricket profiles to further the New Day cause. It's much more important than any sponsorship deal could ever be. We want to make the future brighter in any way we can.

The future is already bright for the Lee boys. Both are set to play significant roles in what lies ahead on the cricket field. Brett has a simple aim:

Whether I only play 10 Tests or 100, I have to have fun. To me, the number one aim is to get more kids playing cricket again. And to do that, players have to look at themselves as entertainers. We're there to try to please the crowd. It shouldn't be hard because basically we are out on the field having fun with our mates. It's such a buzz playing for your country, and if I can come across on TV to kids as someone who is enjoying himself, hopefully we'll get a few more boys and girls out in the backyard again.

Cricket is just a game. I'm just very lucky that I am paid for playing it, but that shouldn't take away what it's all about. Whether we get paid or not, we still have to smile, laugh, and have a good time. I reckon I'd play Test cricket for nothing. But don't tell that to the ACB!

Even now I still find it nearly impossible to believe that I'm playing cricket with my childhood idols. I suppose in many ways I'm still just a kid. I hope I never lose that approach to the game. I have had my problems with injuries, and I must accept that I'll probably get more somewhere down the track. Because of that I have to make the most of every game I play. At this stage I don't have any statistical aims. Maybe in a few years from now I will, but for the moment I just want to help Australia stay at the top. If personal milestones come along as well, then I'll have another reason to celebrate.

Although I'm only really at the beginning of my career, cricket has already been good to me. Bowling fast for Australia is all I've ever wanted to do. So, I have to make the most of it while I can. I'm really excited about what is ahead.

Shane is at a different stage of his career. After playing nearly a decade in the first-class arena he still believes the best years lie ahead, but also realises now is the time to think about life after cricket. In 2000 he joined the international company Sporting Frontiers as a project director. Under Neil Maxwell and non-executive director Steve Waugh, the company established a cricketing arm that is involved in developing cricket, both in the domestic game and on the subcontinent. As a result, Shane's time has been divided between playing for Australia, leading NSW, and thinking about where cricket may head long after he's retired:

Like every game, cricket must evolve with the times. One thing that may happen — and I'd really like to see it happen — is the development of international franchises — whether it be countries, states, or superclubs. If developed sensibly, it would be a good way to expand the game into new countries. It would obviously take away some of the tradition, but we must continually think about what's happening outside our own game. If we don't, other sports will go past us.

It's not impossible to think that cricket will one day be like England's Premier League soccer, with transfers in place and Australian players scattered all over the globe. If you look at clubs like Manchester United and Chelsea you'll find there are very few home-grown stars, yet they are very successful clubs that have helped the promotion of soccer on a worldwide scale.

The evolution of cricket to such an extent may be a way off yet, and such a thing may never happen, but nothing would surprise me. It wasn't that long ago that no-one had heard of one-day cricket.

Even during my time the game has changed. It's a lot more intense now than when I started. That's because there's more money involved, and players are now full-time cricketers. It's their livelihood, but we must never forget we are still playing a game. There is also much more public scrutiny. Because of the match-fixing scandal cricket's image has copped a caning lately, so it's every current player's responsibility to rebuild credibility.

But there are some issues that the media makes too much of. Sledging is one of them. More sledging goes on in Shield cricket than in international cricket by a long way. In all the one-dayers I've played against England, I can't remember there ever being a word against me. The West Indians don't say anything, and you never know whether the Pakistanis or Indians are or not. Most of the time it's pretty harmless. And in fact many of the best sledges are funny. Before I really knew him, Brad McNamara got me with a good one during a grade match early on in my career. I nicked one to the keeper, but didn't walk. I looked up and there was Brad staring at me saying, 'You're f . . . ing kidding mate. I could pull splinters out of that ball and build a billy cart. Why aren't you walking?'

Merv Hughes could be bad. He'd mumble a lot of stuff, and huff and puff, snort and sniff. He could be pretty intimidating, but again it was the funny ones that left their mark. I can remember NSW batsman Kevin Roberts had this unusual habit of facing the keeper when he took centre at the start of an innings. One day Robbo was scratching his mark, and from the top of his run up about 40 metres away Merv yelled, 'Hey mate, don't forget I'm bowling from this end.' I'm not saying sledging is a necessary part of the game, but it is acceptable. I admit I sledge, but I definitely try to pick my mark because there are some guys who are more susceptible to it than others.

From a personal point of view, I still have a lot more to give to the game and a lot more to prove. I've shown I can make it as a bowler in one-day cricket, and I've contributed when I can with the bat. My goal is to become a world-class all-rounder, respected everywhere as someone who can win a game. I'm not a great fan of the word 'potential', but I know I haven't lived up to mine yet. The fact that Brett's doing so well has inspired me no end. There is still the dream that one day we will play a Test together. Dreams have already taken us a long way from Mount Warrigal.

CHAPTER TWENTY

BROTHERLY VIEWS

SHANE ON BRETT

Expressing my feelings is something that doesn't come as easy to me as hitting a cricket ball. So to write my personal views about someone I love is a difficult task. Brett has come a long way from the backyard games in Mount Warrigal, but not without his setbacks. Two broken backs, spurs on his ankles, and a broken arm haven't affected his determination and hunger to succeed.

I know I have been harder on Brett than anyone else in my life. I don't know if this is just a big brother syndrome, or if I'm just being overprotective. I would hate to see him make the same mistakes I've already made. He is generous, caring, loyal, dedicated, and has a great sense of humour. His personality is infectious, and makes me feel as if I'm 13 again, but he can sometimes be the most frustrating person on earth because his personality is so similar to mine in many ways.

I remember Dad trying to get Brett to do his homework one night. This was a regular occurrence that always ended in tears and frustration. Dad would leave Brett in his room with his head buried deep in textbooks, only to come in 10 minutes later to see Brett flat on his back watching television. On one occasion Dad confronted Brett with: 'What do you want to be in life?' Brett replied in his usual cheeky manner by quoting an Australian rugby union television advertisement that was running at the time. He said, 'I want to be a Wallaby.' Dad was furious, but I think he may have forgiven Brett now that he has become successful in another sport!

When we were growing up, everything at home was competitive. From the push-bike races around the house, to the tackle footy in the nearby park, to the thousands of games of cricket in the driveway. The games would coincide with the seasons and the sports on television at that particular time. One day Brett would be Robert de Castella, the next Garry Jack.

Although we are very similar in many ways, we do have our different interests. Brett has a real love of outdoor sports such as fishing and shooting. This love of hunting was evident from a young age. I remember him sitting for hours alone just inside the back door holding a piece of string that ran from the door over a tree branch and suspended a brick above the ground. Breadcrumbs were strategically placed on the ground to lure unsuspecting birds into the target zone. I don't think Brett ever actually squashed a bird with this unusual method, but it might resemble the patience and tactics he uses on the cricket field to dismiss batsmen today!

When Brett was growing up, self-confidence was an issue. His two front teeth were knocked out in a trailer accident in the backyard when he was five. He was shattered. And he considered himself short for his age, and would measure himself daily on the back of his bedroom door to see if he had grown. Since then he has grown a lot, and I now consider him a very confident and knowledgeable individual.

He is one of my best mates. He is a great sounding board, giving me honest opinions in all facets of life. I love playing cricket with him because it is nearly always fun, and Brett's presence inspires me to succeed. We aren't jealous of each other, and enjoy each other's successes. I'm very proud to say he is my brother.

BRETT ON SHANE

I have never been asked to write about Shane before. Sure, I've been asked a million questions about him. What's he like? Do we both get on well? Who's the better cricketer? It's not until I've had to sit down and put pen to paper that I've realised it's not as easy as it looks.

The one word I would use to sum up Shane is 'honesty'. He is always straight to the point. Generally that's an advantage because you know exactly where you stand. If I ever need to know anything I simply ask Shane, and he tells me how it is.

I have always looked up to Shane. He played for Australia first, so he proved it could be done. He has helped me so much along the way that I would even say if it wasn't for him I would never have played Test cricket. He's a bit like a manager/mentor/best mate all rolled into one. I can see now why he must have got the shits with me when we were growing up because here I was always dragging along next to him, probably annoying him to death. I wanted to do what he did, just to be cool like him.

It was great growing up with Shane and Grant. Both are very special brothers to me, but we sure had our hard times when we played all those games of sport in the backyard.

Shane was always very protective. He kept an eye out for me and never let anyone push me around. He always made sure that I was OK, no matter what I was doing.

Shane is also a big softy, but growing up he'd never admit that to us because he always wanted to have the tough big brother image. For example, he'd never admit to us whenever he had a girlfriend. He would say stuff like, 'Nah, I haven't got a girlfriend. Come on mate. Ya gotta be kidding.'

Deep down inside he is a very caring person who always puts the family first. He is a great role model for kids, and especially me. I am very proud of him, and consider myself very lucky to have such a great bloke as my older brother.

About the Author

James Knight was raised in the country town of Gunnedah in north west NSW. From a young age he spent endless hours bashing a cricket ball into a chicken-wire fence in the backyard of the family property. When he realised he'd never be good enough to play for Australia, he dreamt of becoming a cricket writer and commentator.

He began his professional career as a cadet journalist for Radio 2DU, Dubbo in 1988. In the past decade his career has spanned Sydney metropolitan radio, press and television. A three-time winner of the NSW Cricket Association's best TV feature, he has covered tours in India, Pakistan, South Africa, the West Indies and England. He has often had the thrill of being called on as an extra net bowler — one of the highlights of his life. He now runs his own production company, KnightWriter Productions, and is currently producing television documentaries and programs in India. This is his first book. In between running marathons he is working on a novel.